SOME FUNDAMENTALS
OF INFORMATION RETRIEVAL

Some Fundamentals of Information Retrieval

JOHN R. SHARP F.L.A.

A GRAFTON BOOK

ANDRE DEUTSCH

FIRST PUBLISHED MARCH 1965 BY
ANDRE DEUTSCH LIMITED
105 GREAT RUSSELL STREET
LONDON WC1
COPYRIGHT © 1965 BY JOHN R SHARP
SECOND IMPRESSION SEPTEMBER 1968
ALL RIGHTS RESERVED
PRINTED IN GREAT BRITAIN BY
CLARKE DOBLE AND BRENDON LTD
PLYMOUTH
SBN 233 95712 X

Preface

The problem of providing for the efficient retrieval of stored information has created a challenge which is attracting the attention of workers from an increasing number of different disciplines. The proliferation of different kinds of approach to the problem has tended to cloud the issue and perhaps the major causes of the present confusion are the disproportionate amount of attention accorded to machines on the one hand and the preoccupation with abstruse theory, particularly mathematical theory, on the other.

This book was born of a conviction that we are losing sight of the significance of many of the principles which can be isolated and exploited within the limits of our present knowledge because of the complex and fluid state in which information retrieval finds itself today. These principles, which to my mind are fundamental to the problem, are the subject of this book, but the first word of the title has been used expressly to intimate that no claim is made to an exhaustive treatment of the subject.

An attempt has been made to provide between one pair of covers a study of the principles of the several kinds of retrieval systems, both conventional and non-conventional, in order to analyse the reasons for the inadequacy of the former and to show how the latter overcome some of the inherent weaknesses of the conventional methods. The principal theme of the book forms a continuing argument through Chapters 1 to 6 and comprises an integrated study of classification, the alphabetical subject index, the simple mathematical theory of concept co-ordination, the several methods of application of co-ordinate principles ranging from optical stencil cards to the computer, and the techniques used to control indexing language in these newer systems.

Chapter 7 discusses the difference between co-ordination and correlation in order to demonstrate the need to clarify our ideas about the place of information retrieval in the wider field of information and data handling and processing and to warn against the danger of confusion arising from trying to build additional facilities into systems when we have not yet mastered our immediate problem. Chapter 8 is a survey of work done on automatic abstracting and automatic indexing, methods which may at some time in the future cause a fundamental shift in the emphasis on the several functions involved in providing for information storage and retrieval.

The book should be equally useful to the student preparing for examinations in librarianship and the newcomer to the information field who needs to assimilate quickly the fundamental principles which ought to govern decisions regarding choice of methods and equipment when the establishment of a retrieval system for a particular purpose is projected. It is perhaps not too much to hope that the experienced worker in the field will also find stimulation in the several novel approaches to both old and new conceptions and that he will be helped to place a difficult subject in better perspective.

The opinions expressed in the book are entirely my own, and I must accept entirely the responsibility for them, but it would be remiss of me not to acknowledge the help which I have derived, often in a very indirect way, from a large number of colleagues. What knowledge I have of the subject has accumulated over a long period of time and much of it stems from discussions which I have had with other workers in the field. Though my views certainly do not coincide with those of many members of the Classification Research Group, the meetings of that group which I attended some years ago were a source of much valuable information. The opportunities which I had of meeting other interested parties during my two-year term with the ASLIB Cranfield Research Project under Cyril Cleverdon's direction were also very valuable and the value of the experience on the Project itself hardly needs any emphasis.

Of the many writers on the subject who have influenced

me, much the most important is John Metcalfe. The reading
of his two books *Information indexing and subject cataloguing*
and *Subject classifying and indexing of libraries and literature*
has been a difficult but rewarding task. I have been somewhat
critical of part of Metcalfe's philosophy, but this does not
detract from the fact that I feel that his work is the most
penetrating analysis made to date of so much of what is
basic to the retrieval problem.

The permission of British Nylon Spinners Limited to have
the book published and to use so much material which has
been derived in the course of my work is greatly appreciated.
I am grateful to my present chief, Wilfred Ashworth, who
carefully read the entire text and whose suggestions resulted
in many alterations, particularly in matters of style; to Mr
A. Cinderey who drew the diagrams; to Mr D. J. S. Morgan
for help with photographic work; and to Mr Alan Venmore
of the Computer Services Section of B.N.S. who has taken
such a keen interest in the project concerning the experimental 'SLIC' index, and who has carried out the work relating
thereto so competently.

I am greatly indebted to Mr James A. Bear, Jr, Curator of
the Thomas Jefferson Memorial Foundation, Charlottesville,
Virginia, for seeking out the letter from Jefferson to his friend
James Ogilvie, which is quoted in Chapter 2. The permission
of Messrs Routledge and Kegan Paul Ltd to reproduce the
passages from Cohen and Nagel's *An introduction to logic*
in Chapter 6 is also gratefully acknowledged.

The work of transcribing a virtually illegible manuscript
into an impeccable typescript was carried out by Miss Janet
Gates and this meant a lessening of the burden of which I
am truly appreciative. Finally, my sincerest thanks are due
to my wife, Grace, not only for her passive contribution in
terms of patience and forbearance, but for her active encour-
agement at times when my enthusiasm for the work seemed
to be flagging.

J. R. S.

Contents

List of Diagrams

I

The Nature of the Problem

The expression 'information retrieval' was coined by Calvin
Mooers in 1950. It is generally taken to embrace the whole
field of the problem of recovering from recorded knowledge
those particular pieces of information which may be needed
at particular times for particular purposes, but though this
implies the inclusion of conventional practices such as classification and cataloguing, there is a tendency to regard the
subject as providing a substitute for methods such as this.
There is, however, no recognisable or accepted body of theory,
let alone practice, which can be considered as an established
discipline. For this reason those writers who have attempted
to survey the field in general, such as Vickery[1] and Fairthorne,[2] have studiously avoided the use of titles which suggest any claim to treatment of a subject whose boundaries
are recognisable. The one exception to this is the book by
Kent.[3] This is a very valuable book, but the principles which
it expounds are not necessarily those which will finally
determine standard methods for information retrieval and the
use of the word 'textbook' in its title seems a little premature.
   The different approaches to the problem which are still
live and more or less vigorously pursued are legion. Even
with conventional methods there are still advocates of the
alphabetico-specific catalogue on the one hand, such as
Metcalfe, and of the classified catalogue, or methods based on
classificatory principles on the other, such as some members
at least of the Classification Research Group in Great Britain.
The philosophies involved here are as diametrically opposed
as ever they were. Some would consider that classification has
now a stronger claim because of the advent of the newer
techniques, whilst their opponents would argue that these

11

developments have added to, rather than reduced the confusion.

Many of the people newly on the scene seem, for better or for worse, to have rejected all that has been propounded in the past and to have devised systems which are expected to work solely because they take advantage of the facilities which certain types of equipment provide. The kinds of equipment being used in the information retrieval field range from the very simple to the very complex and we have seen the advent of the use of punched cards, both edge-punched and field-punched, both for sequential scanning on the 'item entry' principle and for superimposition for detecting coincidence of holes on the 'term entry' principle, of the system of posting document numbers visually to 'feature cards', of special machines such as the Rapid Selector, Filmsort and Minicard equipment, and of the use of computers.

Additionally we have the pure theorists who concern themselves entirely with principles and seek to solve the problem first on paper, with the hope that equipment can be designed and built to put theory into practice. The present state of affairs in this respect is anything but encouraging, for there seems to be a great gulf fixed between theory and the prospect of its being applied to practical solutions. In all sciences there must inevitably be a considerable lag before the effects of research are seen in application, but in the field of information retrieval the problems are so complex and the investigations being made currently cover so many facets of the subject, some of them apparently very marginal, that it is hard to discern any trend in a particular direction, and the chance of lighting accidentally on a solution to the problem as a whole seems remote because of the piecemeal nature of the attempts at a solution. It is probable, however, that a great deal of wasted effort has gone into the design of equipment (popularly called 'hardware') for it is evident that in many cases of the use of machines for retrieval, the fundamental problems of subject designation have been largely ignored, presumably because machines are considered to be capable of eliminating the problems rather than solving them. This approach has no doubt been encouraged by the existence of machines which have been designed for other purposes but whose versatility makes them an attractive proposition from the point of view of the documentalist. An attack on the problem theoretically is undoubtedly essential, for providing the problems of classification, of specification, of coding, of semantics, or whatever else might be found to be relevant are solved, it seems unlikely that the problem of building the machines will defeat the engineer.

A remarkable state of affairs seems to exist in the United States, where an enormous amount of money has been spent on 'hardware', and a thesis by Gerald Jahoda,[4] published in 1960, is very revealing in this respect. Jahoda lists ten reasons why certain organisations changed from using one kind of information retrieval system to another, and under no less than eight of the ten heads there are cases where an organisation changed from system A to system B and another changed from system B to system A for exactly the same reason! This seems to suggest some fault in the philosophy behind retrieval systems and one suspects that far too many decisions on the choice of systems are made by a consideration of the physical equipment available rather than by considering the nature of the particular retrieval problem which exists. There are certain very elementary principles which underlie the methods for meeting various requirements and the state of affairs which Jahoda has revealed shows that these are largely ignored when decisions regarding choice of systems are made. Another important feature of the present situation is the contradiction between the philosophy which argues for the adoption of systems which provide for 'concept co-ordination', a facility lacking in conventional systems, and the now widespread use of KWIC indexing, which is a mechanised form of the crude title-word indexing practised a century ago.

In many cases the decision on the adoption of a particular system may clearly be a question of choice between several non-conventional systems, because circumstances dictate requirements which only methods such as this can meet, but all too often the choice is falsely considered to be so limited because of the assumption that conventional systems are now entirely outmoded. It would obviously be a mistake to try to preserve what can be proved to have been superseded, for progress in this field is likely to suffer just as much as it would in any other field by a tendency to be conservative. There is no doubt that some of the newer techniques which have been developed are infinitely better solutions to some if not all of our problems than the conventional methods. It seems however that the pendulum has swung much too far, for careful consideration of some of the principles which have been used in the past can provide useful guidance in the development of newer methods, and the least that such consideration can do is to improve the quality of the reasoning behind the change from the old to the new.

Information retrieval systems can take many different physical forms, ranging from the simple card index to computer-based installations, and the principles on which their functioning is based can also vary widely in detail if not basically, but the fundamental problem which is common to all is that of providing for the nearest possible coincidence between the description of a subject by a searcher and the description used to enter documents on that subject in the system. In a perfect system we would have the position in which every relevant document would be retrieved when a search was made, without the production of a single irrelevant document. In practice we cannot economically achieve the first part of this requirement, for we cannot yet design systems which will certainly retrieve every relevant document, though we could achieve this by the procedure of searching the whole file, perhaps the file of the documents themselves, every time a search is made. We might achieve the second part of this requirement, or at least approach it closely, by highly specific subject designation, but the cost of this, unless a much more sophisticated method of designation than is available at present were to be used, is likely to be a poor standard of retrieval of relevant documents.

The parameters referred to here are known as 'recall factor' and 'pertinency factor', expressions due to Perry, Kent and

Berry,[5] though Cleverdon uses the expressions 'recall ratio' and 'relevance ratio'.[6] Recall factor is the ratio between the number of relevant documents which are retrieved in a search and the number which *ought* to be retrieved, i.e. the total number of documents in the system which are relevant. Pertinency factor is the ratio between the number of relevant documents which are retrieved in a search and the total number retrieved.

These two parameters are the main criteria of the efficiency of a system, and we normally aim to have both these values as high as possible. Practical considerations limit them, however, for in the present state of the art it is impossible to reach perfection, and new systems are usually created on a largely empirical basis, with a view to attaining a reasonable standard of general performance. There is little evidence of conscious effort to design systems meeting performance requirements specified by these criteria, though differing circumstances may demand greater emphasis on the one factor than on the other. In one set of conditions we may insist that recall be virtually 100 per cent, regardless of the cost in terms of irrelevant documents retrieved, and an apparently uneconomic system of this kind may in fact be a sound economic proposition in, say, an overall research activity where the cost of exhaustive retrieval may be negligible compared with the saving accruing from the non-repetition of even occasional pieces of expensive work. Other circumstances may be such that individual pieces of information are readily found, each in several sources, and the retrieval of but one such source is always adequate to meet a request. Emphasis here might well be placed on pertinency factor at the expense of recall factor.

Another question which some consider must be taken into account is that a particular system may be intended to serve one or other of the two different requirements generally known as 'specific reference' and 'generic survey'. There has long been an idea that readers in libraries fall into two categories: those who require a specific piece of information about a specific subject, and those who wish to study a subject in all its ramifications, and perhaps even to explore its so-called 'related subjects'. There is little evidence to substantiate this conception, but on the assumption that these two distinct groups of readers exist, opinions have been expressed about the suitability of the various types of retrieval system to meet the two kinds of requirement. Some claim that the classified catalogue serves the purpose of generic survey better, whilst the alphabetico-specific catalogue is better for specific reference. Others go no further than to say that the needs of both types of enquirer cannot be met in a single system. In special libraries, however, it is probably true to say that we are concerned to a much larger extent with specific reference than we are with generic survey. The specialist is usually concerned with problems relating to a quite specific area of knowledge, and even when he wishes to have every bit of information which can be found on a particular subject, i.e. when he wishes to survey a particular subject generically, the subject is usually so specific that the approach can hardly be considered to be anything but 'specific reference'. It might be better to regard the difference between specific reference and generic survey as one of degree rather than one of principle, particularly as there is relative extent not only between what is regarded as specific in one field compared with another, but also between the subject fields covered by different classification schemes. It is not admitted for the purpose of the discussion in this book that it is impossible to have retrieval systems which will cater for both requirements, but in general it will be assumed that the aim is provision for specific reference, for it is the increasing complexity of subjects dealt with in literature which has precipitated the crisis in documentation and the retrieval of subjects of such complexity can hardly be considered to be anything but a problem of specific reference.

Metcalfe has stated that 'Only known names in a known order . . . will indicate information'.[7] The inference here is that the knowledge of the name of a particular subject, and of the arrangement of the file in which entries are stored, is common to indexer and searcher. Metcalfe does not state that this is all that is necessary for information retrieval purposes but contends that all systems must *start* with known names in a known order, mentioning not only the alphabetical catalogue, which is nothing but known names in a known order, but also the alphabetical index to the classified catalogue and the alphabetical index to codings for mechanical selection. Nevertheless the theme of his book is an argument in favour of the alphabetico-specific catalogue, and there must be recognition of the limitations of the principle in this restricted sense as far as its application to current storage and retrieval problems is concerned.

Known names such as CATS or CAMS are sufficiently distinctive and exclusive, and alphabetical order so well-known, that the storage of entries for information on these subjects provides for certain and instant location of entries for relevant documents. In many fields of library and information work, however, we are concerned with subjects which do not lend themselves to designations as simple as this and to talk of 'known names', at least in the special library field, is a gross oversimplification of the problem, for a subject may be the aggregate of a considerable number of individual elemental concepts, the naming of each of these elements may be subject to problems of synonymity and questions of indicating relationships between elements may arise. The solution to the problem of ensuring coincidence in subject naming between indexer and searcher rests on the formulation of principles which govern the nature of subject designations and the drawing up of rules based on these principles which will ensure that the same designation for a given subject is always the final product of the application of the rules to the naming of that subject.

As far as 'known order' is concerned it must be said at once that though subjects may need to be provided with 'known names' in the sense discussed above, i.e. names which are unique, though arrived at only by the application of rules, and not necessarily by merely being called to mind, 'known order' in the main file, as distinct from auxiliary indexes, is not essential. There are available systems of many kinds, always involving a machine of some kind, though it may be only a pack of cards and a knitting needle, which permit the filing of entries in random order, the finding of entries being achieved by examining every entry to determine whether the designation of the document matches that selected for search. It is true, as Metcalfe claims, that mechanical searching must be preceded by the use of a list of known names in a known order, but the use of this list is limited to providing access to the individual components which comprise a complex subject description and in the field of information work which is concerned with such complex subject concepts, it can be said that not only is a 'known order' in the main store of a system unnecessary, but because of the impracticability of storing the necessary number of entries, the principle must be rejected, at least insofar as it means the finding of a known name at one point in a known order. The reasons for this will be dealt with in chapter 4.

Regardless of this question of order, there are basically two ways in which we can handle subjects for the purpose of recording documents in a retrieval system and recovering such documents or their addresses by interrogating the system. One method is that mentioned above, i.e. the naming of the subject, however complex, detailed and specific it may be, with provision for ensuring that there will be adequate matching between subject designation at searching and that at indexing. The 'name' actually applied to the subject can be a code representing the name if the system requires that a code be used, but this is not to be construed as being the same as classifying the subject. Proper handling of subject designation is the crux of the matter, whether 'known order' or any other principle be the basis of locating relevant entries.

The other method is to 'classify', the principle here being that subjects are entered in the system, and recovered, on the basis of relative position in the scheme of things, and in theory at least it is not necessary even to name the subject. The next two chapters will be devoted to classification and alphabetical subject cataloguing respectively, these being the conventional practical manifestations of the two methods. There are excellent textbooks on both these subjects and the intention here is merely to outline the principles in order to provide a basis for discussion of the pros and cons of their applicability to the problems currently facing us.

REFERENCES

1 Vickery, B. C. *On retrieval system theory*, Butterworths, London, 1961.
2 Fairthorne, R. A. *Towards information retrieval*, Butterworths, London, 1961.
3 Kent, A. *Textbook on mechanized information retrieval*, Interscience, New York, 1962.
4 Jahoda, G. *Correlative indexing systems for the control of research records*. Columbia University, D. L. S. thesis, 1960. University Microfilms Mic 60-3082.
5 Perry, J. W., Kent, A. and Berry, M. M. *Machine literature searching*, Interscience, New York, 1956, p. 43.
6 Cleverdon, C. W. *ASLIB Cranfield Research Project: Report on the testing and analysis of an investigation into the comparative efficiency of indexing systems*. Cranfield, October 1962, p. 70.
7 Metcalfe, J. *Information indexing and subject cataloguing: alphabetical: classified: co-ordinate: mechanical*. Scarecrow Press, New York, 1957, p. 28.

Classification

Classification as it has been expounded over the past fifty years in textbooks written for students of librarianship is not an easy subject. This is due in no small measure to the fact that the theory is based on the principles of classification which derive from logic and it is exceedingly difficult to reconcile what is taken as it stands out of the context of logic with what we try to do when we apply classification for bibliographical purposes. Logical principles are undoubtedly very helpful, but though differences are stressed between classifications of 'knowledge' and classifications of 'books' the limitations of logic are seldom recognised.

Logic can be said to be the study of the validity of inference, or more simply but perhaps more crudely, the soundness of argument. It concerns itself with the ways in which conclusions can be drawn from premises, and it is limited to just this, for the truth of the premises, that is whether what the premises assert bears any relation to actual fact, does not affect the soundness of the argument based on the premises. Thus the validity of the argument is the point at issue, not the truth of the premises, nor indeed of the conclusions. Logic has done its work when it has established that if a premise is true then the conclusion must be true.

It is clear that logic is concerned with making statements about things. It affirms or denies one thing of another and the unit which it uses to do this is the proposition. The simplest proposition consists of two terms joined by the 'copula'. One term is the subject of the proposition, i.e. that about which the affirmation or denial is made, and the other is the predicate, i.e. that which is affirmed or denied of the subject. The copula is the present tense of the verb 'to be'.

Any simple statement such as 'All metals are conductors' is a proposition and in fact the definition of a proposition is 'anything that can significantly be said to be true or false'.

One very important type of argument used in logic is what is known as the 'syllogism'. The definition given by Luce will serve: 'A syllogism is a triad of connected propositions, so related that one of them, called the Conclusion, necessarily follows from the other two, which are called the Premises'.[1] If we use the proposition 'All metals are conductors' and another proposition 'All copper alloys are metals', we have two premises from which we can draw the conclusion 'All copper alloys are conductors'. We have inferred the conclusion from what is stated in the premises. This particular form of argument is introduced here as it serves to show clearly how logic uses classification for its purposes. If we imagine a class of things which are metals and a class of things which are conductors of electricity, we can easily imagine, from the first premise, that the former class is entirely included in the latter. We can also see from the second premise, that the class of things which are copper alloys is entirely included in the class of things which are metals. This means that the class 'copper alloys' is entirely included in the class 'conductors' and it can therefore be asserted that 'All copper alloys are conductors'. This is one of several kinds of logical relation between classes, i.e. inclusion, partial inclusion, exclusion and coincidence, which can be displayed diagrammatically by the use of Euler circles. Stebbing[2] gives a clear and concise account of their mode of application. Our particular syllogism would be represented as shown in Figure 1.

It is clear that relations between classes serve logic's particular purpose, i.e. they enable us to affirm or deny a predicate of a subject by virtue of the one being included in, partially included in, excluded from, or coincident with the other. Indeed it may be said that Aristotelean logic, with its concentration on the subject-predicate relationship is a study of the relationships between classes. However, the last century has seen the development of another kind of logic, which pursues the same objectives, but which introduces the principles of mathematics. Because this logic uses symbols in a way similar to that in which algebra uses them (not exactly the same way, be it noted), it has become known as 'symbolic logic' and is considered to comprise a set of calculi, including the calculus of classes, which treat the subject more widely and more rigorously.

An important aspect of the treatment of classes becomes

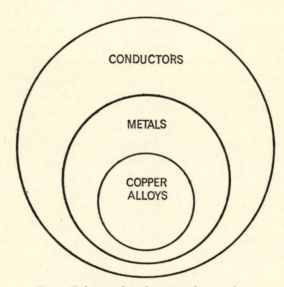

Fig 1 Euler circles showing class inclusion

explicit in the calculus of classes for it introduces the idea of operations on classes in addition to dealing with relations. This can hardly be considered to have been dealt with even implicitly in traditional logic. Cohen and Nagel sum up the two concepts: 'The difference between operations upon classes and relations between classes is this: operations upon classes yield classes; the assertions of relations between classes are propositions, not classes.'[3] In other words logical operations on classes define new classes and the relations between classes represent statements, or propositions. In books on symbolic logic, the two are treated quite separately, e.g. in Lee,[4] where separate chapters are devoted to the two principles.

Diagrams are used for illustrating operations in a fashion similar to that used for illustrating relations, and the type used is usually the circles devised by the English logician John Venn. The operations concerned are those of conjunction, disjunction and negation, which are sometimes spoken of as logical multiplication, logical addition and logical subtraction. Thus if we have a class of red things and a class of square things, multiplication will give us the 'logical product', a new class of things which are both red and square. Addition will give us the 'logical sum', a new class of things which are either red or square and subtraction will give us the 'logical differ-ence', a new class of things which are red, but specifically not square. (Venn diagrams illustrating these several operations will be found at the beginning of chapter 5, where they are used in connection with the discussion on co-ordinate index-ing.) To distinguish between relations as we have illustrated them with Euler circles, and operations as illustrated by Venn diagrams, we should think of the two concepts in the follow-ing way. In the case of relations, if we take a particular area, we have a class which we have already defined and we can say certain things about that class according to its being included in, partially included in or excluded from another class as shown by the areas. In the case of operations, a particular area defines what the class is, according to what that area is made up of, i.e. according to which classes are associated to form that area.

We have thus isolated two separate things which logic can do for us. Firstly, it can help us to argue more rationally, to be surer of the validity of the way in which we draw con-clusions from evidence which we have. Secondly it helps us in the process of the formation of classes. Now those who have introduced the principles of classification which derive from logic into the field of bibliographical classification have assumed that when logic talks of genus, species, etc. and relations between classes, it is concerned with arrangement between classes. The idea seems to be given some support in textbooks of logic themselves, because these often mention classification in the fields of botany and zoology, but the purpose of this type of classification coincides exactly with logic's own purpose, that is it tries to provide new knowledge by drawing conclusions from what is already known or thought to be known. It is not interested in the physical arrangement of specimens, but the intellectual process of deducing what is not already known from observations of relations between classes. Wolf makes this clear when he states 'Classification is a method of science, it is a way of knowing or regarding things. It is primarily an intellectual activity, not a physical activity. The classification may be exemplified or illustrated by the grouping of objects in a museum for instance. But the physical grouping is not the real, essential classification: it is only an illustration of it. The essence of classification consists in the fact that certain things are thought of as related in certain ways to one another.'[5]

There is more of this in Wolf, and other textbooks on the subject provide no ground for believing that logicians have ever intended to convey the idea that the concept of relationship means anything other than class inclusion for the purpose of inference. As far as the making of classes is concerned, as was stated above, traditional logic has not concerned itself with logical operations as has the newer symbolic logic, but it would not be true to say that it has never been concerned with class making, for 'definition' has received some attention and inasmuch as definition has been considered to be the same as connotation it is the same as class making, for connotation means the sum of the attributes which determine a class, and the eligibility or otherwise of things for membership of the class is decided by it. Indeed it might be argued that definition is an important aspect of classification in the context of traditional logic, for it is treated as part and parcel of it, and even more significant is the fact that of the five predicables, (which are discussed later in this chapter) the one we know as 'species' was known in the doctrine of Aristotle as 'definition', until the substitution was made by the Greek philosopher Porphyry.

Now the point of all this is that the two things which we have discussed, i.e. class-making and logical relations do not provide us with a complete basis for bibliographical classification. Class-making we must have of course because we have to assign the subjects of documents to classes to which they properly belong, but it is not always possible to create classes by logical principles. By no stretch of the imagination can the main classes of general classification schemes such as Dewey be said to be derived from a genus by any principle belonging to logic, and whilst logical division can be recognised at particular points in such schemes, this non-logical division is much in evidence, even down to the most specific levels. So that logic, though it can provide for class-making by rigorous methods for its own purposes, cannot provide us with a universal method for generating classes which will give us an hierarchical arrangement of the subject matter of even a comparatively narrow field. And when we have our classes, even though they may be the result of perfect logical division, logic has nothing to offer us in the way of determining the order in which those classes shall be arranged. If we take the class 'engineering' and divide it into the various species of engineering such as hydraulic, mechanical, electrical, aeronautical, etc., criteria other than logical ones must determine that order. The logical relation of class inclusion has determined that the species shall be so located as to be shown to be subordinate to the genus, but this is as far as it goes. We are left with the need to provide an overall arrangement of classes, taking into account this one type of relation which logic determines for us, and it is the principle of arrangement between classes which marks off bibliographical classification from classification in logic. Metcalfe sums up the difference thus: 'Classification in logic is not classifying or classing in the wool classing or book classifying senses; it is not the examination of individuals for their distribution over already established classes. The word is made up of the Latin word for class, which is ours, and the Latin word for making, and originally it meant simply the making or setting up of classes; in logic it means this, and may also mean an arrangement of classes, but although this use of the name is recognised in logic, logic is hardly interested in class arrangement.'[6]

It is the arrangement of the multitude of classes with which we are faced when we classify a subject field for bibliographical purposes which gives such classification its value, for it is the relative position of things on such a 'map' which serves both purposes (a) of finding a particular subject by its being known to be located in a particular area of the scheme and (b) of grouping together those subjects which the user will find it advantageous to have at one position. The idea of the significance of the relative position of classes was recognised by Wright when he said of classification: 'It also has the ability to indicate meaning through position when there is no brief individual name for a subject.'[7] Relative position is the fundamental question whether a subject has a brief individual name or not, but Wright did appreciate that bibliographical classification should observe this principle. Obviously for providing for the placing of an unnamed subject in any scheme of things or for the converse process of implying the nature of such a subject by its position something more than mere class-making and class-naming is required and only classification with a clear display of relative position between classes can do this. If we are to argue the pros and cons of classification in the bibliographical sense we must be careful not to invoke definitions and principles from logic and quote them as though their context is that of bibliographical classification, for classification in logic is not synonymous with classification in the bibliographical field.

It is not surprising that there should arise out of this the controversial issue of whether classification schemes should follow a 'natural order' or 'the order of the sciences'. When logic, which provides a useful method, leaves a large part of the problem of arrangement still to be settled, it is understandable that philosophers should seek an order for the overall scheme of things and the classification schemes such as that of Francis Bacon resulted from such enquiries. Scientists have sought such order in narrower fields, for their purposes also can be furthered by the discovery of such order and it is easy to see the wisdom of this by reference to very modern books in the field of zoology, botany, etc. Such a book is *The algae* by Chapman,[8] the very first chapter of which is entitled 'Classification'. Classification pervades the whole of this book and its purpose is clearly to further under-standing of the book's subject and to provide a basis for the discovery of new knowledge. Further evidence of the applica-tion of classification in this way is the report on a recent conference sponsored by ASLIB at which people concerned with the natural sciences discussed it from this point of view.[9]

The inevitable result of these approaches to the problem by philosophers and scientists seeking tools for their own trades has been that those interested in problems of biblio-graphical classification have argued for or against 'natural order' in bibliographical schemes. On the one hand we have those such as Richardson[10] who argue strongly in favour of trying to make bibliographical schemes follow the order of the sciences and on the other those such as Hulme[11] who take the opposite view, whilst Bliss[12] based his scheme on the 'scientific and educational concensus,' that is the arrangement which conformed most closely to the views of experts in their respective fields. The Library of Congress, though its scheme in outline owes something to the *Expansive classification* of Charles Ammi Cutter,[13] adopted the procedure of arranging the books which comprised its stock in that order which suited them best from the point of view of the actual usage of books and the order is therefore empirically derived. More recently the theories of faceted classification have introduced the principle of 'preferred order' amongst categories, which again provides for the adoption of an order which best suits the purpose in hand, and whilst Ranganathan bases his theories on the 'five fundamental categories' of Personality, Matter, Energy, Space and Time, the idea of 'natural order' finds no place in his writings.

It is probably true to say that as far as the natural sciences are concerned some following of the order recognised there is inevitable. In many other cases the order within limited areas is easily ascertained. In the field of hydraulic engineering for instance, the arrangement of physical things such as Pipework, Closures, Valves, Butterfly valves in that order is self-determining. In the field of information retrieval in special fields however, the issue is frequently nothing like so clear cut, and the very great difficulty of meeting requirements in such cases is dealt with in chapter 4.

Classification in the sense in which it is used in logic is much nearer to the idea of definition or description and it might more properly be considered in relation to the alternative method of dealing with subjects for the purposes of information retrieval which was cited at the end of the last chapter. It is probable that classificatory principles can be useful for the purpose of subject designation and we might well consider this kind of classification as being subject 'specification' rather than subject classification. By specification we mean here the accurate, unambiguous and consistent designation of a subject without reference to its relative position in a classification scheme. It seems paradoxical that Ranganathan, whose disciples pay so much attention to 'helpful order' and whose principles underlie so much current thinking on the formulation of bibliographical classification schemes, should have defined library classification as: '. . . the translation of the name of the subject of a book into a preferred artificial language of ordinal numbers, and the individualisation of the several books dealing with the same specific subject by means of a further set of ordinal numbers which represent some features of the book other than their thought content. The first of these ordinal numbers is called the Class Number of the book. The second ordinal number is called its Book Number.' Ranganathan also says: 'Library classification means the reduction of subjects and books to ordinal numbers for specific purposes.'[14] This sort of definition is nearer to subject specification than to subject classification and there is perhaps not so much paradox as there seems to be, for it may well be that the theories which Ranganathan has propounded have more useful application in subject specifying than they have in the now accepted form (at least by some in Great Britain and elsewhere) of faceted classification with chain index.

The principles of bibliographical classification which have formed the basis of the syllabus for examination by the Library Association in Great Britain for many years are those expounded in textbooks such as Phillips[15] and Sayers.[16, 17] The theories put forward here are those derived from Aristotelean logic and though, as shown above, their effect is more limited than librarians have conceded, they still have much value. In these works the process of classification-making is described as being one of division, that is the breaking down of the field to be classified, according to rules whose purpose is to ensure a systematic procedure and a resulting scheme which satisfies recognised criteria. These criteria are seen at their most formal in the 'canons' of Sayers, which he first propounded in 1907, but which he later modified, and which are currently regarded as of little value, particularly as the methods of analysis of a subject field now available are so much more rigorous. The well-known 'Five Predicables' are the basis of such division and Phillips states that 'The principles laid down in the Predicables govern all classification, for all division proceeds by the addition of differences to the genera.'[18] The Five Predicables are as follows:

Genus   A class of things which is capable of division into two or more sub-groups, which are called 'Species'.

Species   Groups resulting from the division of a genus, each of which may itself become a genus subject to further division.

Difference   An attribute, which, when used to qualify a genus produces a species.

Property   A quality possessed by each species of a genus but which is not peculiar to the members of that genus. Though not essential to the definition of the species, the possession of a property is inherent in the nature of a species.

Accident   A quality which may or may not be possessed by any species of a genus. It is not necessary to the definition of a species, and its existence cannot be inferred by the definition. It can, however, be used, and is used in practice, as a difference.

We might illustrate the application of these principles by a simple example. The class of things called 'military aeroplanes' might be divided in many different ways, but we can demonstrate the principle well enough by a crude breakdown on the principles of 'purpose', 'number of engines' and 'wing position'. These latter are called the 'characteristics' of division and are the bases by which the 'differences' are derived. We begin with the 'summum genus' that is the all-including class, which in this case is 'military aeroplanes', and by application of the characteristic 'purpose' we might derive the differences 'fighting', 'bombing' and 'transport'. Each of these added to the genus 'military aeroplanes' gives us a species of the genus. Thus we have 'military aeroplanes', plus 'fighting' which gives us the species 'fighters' and similarly we have the species 'bombers' and 'transport aircraft'. Each of these species now becomes a genus which is subject to further division and on applying the characteristic 'number of engines' we arrive at the species 'single engined fighters', 'twin engined bombers', etc. Applying the third characteristic, wing position, we arrive at the 'infima species' as far as this crude classification goes, i.e. the final species to be derived, and we have species such as 'twin engined mid-wing bombers', etc. The 'tree' or 'hierarchy' thus produced appears as in figure 2.

It is essential that one characteristic only be used at each step of the division and this must be exhausted before another is introduced. The next characteristic is then used to divide the species so derived to form sub-species, and all the resulting classes are then mutually exclusive. The non-observance of this rule produces collateral classes, i.e. classes of the same order, which are not mutually exclusive, resulting in the

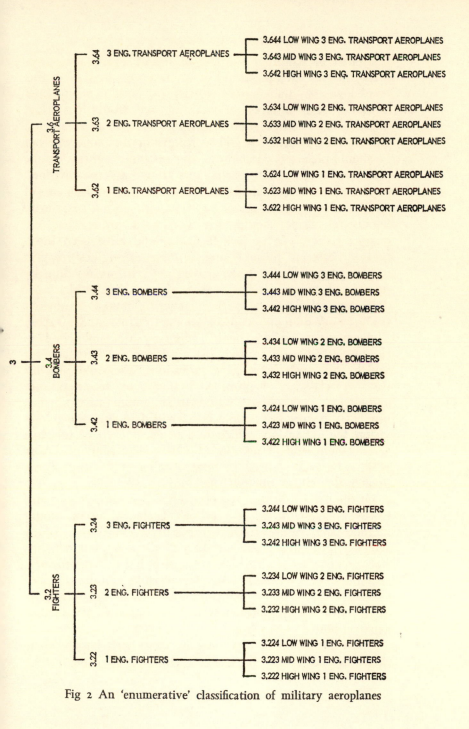

Fig 2 An 'enumerative' classification of military aeroplanes

possibility of assigning a subject to any of several alternative places in the scheme. If, at the first step of division in this breakdown we had derived species by both characteristics 'purpose' and 'number of engines', we would have had 'fighters' and 'single-engined aircraft' as collateral species. Obviously, a classifier would then have doubt about whether he should place a document on 'single-engined fighters' in one place or the other. This is the fault known as 'cross-division'.

This classification fails to meet some of the requirements of an ideal classification. Amongst others, it does not necessarily 'modulate' as it should, for we might argue that the characteristic 'type of propulsion' should have been inter- polated between 'purpose' and 'number of engines', to give us 'jet propelled', 'propeller driven', etc. before dividing by number of engines. It is also certainly not exhaustive, i.e. it does not include every species of every genus, as is obvious from the omission of 'reconnaissance aeroplanes' under 'types'. The contravention of either of these two rules could result in the impossibility of properly placing items in the scheme for which there was no specific provision. We could not, for instance, classify 'jet propelled fighters', or 'reconnaissance aeroplanes'. This could be serious in an 'enumerative' scheme, but both eventualities could be provided for by proper pro- vision for expansion, which is a problem both of schedule arrangement and of notation. Such modifications can more readily be incorporated in faceted schemes because of the greater flexibility inherent therein.

Of the five predicables, two have not so far been mentioned in this breakdown. A 'property' of this class of aircraft might be their being subject to the effect of drag. This is an attribute which is possessed by all members of the class, but which is not peculiar to it, in that birds also have this property. Examples of 'accidents' are 'serviceable', 'unserviceable', 'armed', 'unarmed', etc. Properties and accidents are equally eligible for use as differences for the purposes of practical classification.

These principles of division have now been largely aban- doned in favour of the newer techniques of classification-making, but familiarity with them is a great advantage from the point of view of clear-thinking about classification and indexing, and though their limitations are severe, it is a mistake to consider that they cannot usefully complement other principles. Whatever else they might be, and however limited, they are certainly not invalid.

The newer techniques of 'facet analysis', propounded by Ranganathan, provide a more easily applied procedure for the making of schedules, and they have the advantage that the material is first collected and then marshalled in the way best suited to the purpose in hand. Thus every aspect to be dealt with, as far as is known up to the point of compiling the schedules, is in evidence, and the classification maker is not in the difficult position of having to anticipate every requirement by spontaneously thinking of every potential need, as he must if he uses the traditional processes.

The technique is briefly as follows. The literature which is to be classified is examined and all the significant terms which it uses are listed. The terms are then examined to determine how they might best be grouped according to their similarities, thus providing a number of 'facets' consisting of terms denoting similar kinds of concept. Thus we might have a list of materials forming a 'materials' facet, another forming a 'processes' facet and so on. Each term in such a facet is called a 'focus'. This part of the process is called 'facet analysis' and a very powerful process it can be for many different purposes, and not just for the formulation of faceted classification schemes of the form usually referred to by this expression.

If we were to examine the literature comprising an aeronautical library, we should discover terms such as Delta, Fighters, Ailerons, Landing, Lift, Rectangular, Drag, Control, Wings, Elliptical, Bombers, Elevators, Lateral, Stability, Repair, Transport Aeroplanes, Twin-Engined, Low-Wing, Single-Engined, Longitudinal, Swept-Forward, High-Wing, Take-Off, Climbing, Design, Mid-Wing, Diving, Three-Engined, Maintenance, Sweptback, Tailplanes, Unswept, Directional, Rudders, Triangular, Fuselages, etc. We can readily recognise terms which belong to the same family, or 'facet'. Obviously Delta, Rectangular, Elliptical, Triangular are 'planforms', i.e. the shapes of wings, tailplanes, etc., Maintenance, Design, are 'operations', and Lateral, Longitudinal, Directional signify 'axes' with regard to control, stability, etc. Marshalling all the terms into facets would result in an arrangement of this kind:

Types of aircraft
Ac   Fighters
Ad   Bombers
Ae   Transport
      aircraft

No. of engines
Cd   Single-
      engined
Cf   Twin-
      engined
Ch   Three-
      engined

Wing position
Ec   High-wing
Ee   Mid-wing
Eg   Low-wing

Parts of aircraft
Gd   Tailplanes
Gf   Wings
Gj   Fuselages

Control surfaces
Gm   Ailerons
Gp   Elevators
Gt   Rudders

Planforms
Je   Delta
Jg   Rectangular
Jh   Elliptical
Jm   Triangular

Position determined relative to an axis
Jq   Swept-back
Js   Swept-
     forward
Jv   Unswept

Aerodynamic problems
Kd   Control
Kf   Stability

Flying operations
Lb   Landing
Lg   Take-off
Lm   Climbing
Lp   Diving

Forces
Mb   Lift
Mf   Drag

Axes
Pd   Lateral
Pf   Longitudinal
Ph   Directional

Operations
Tb   Design
Tf   Maintenance
Tj   Repair

It is clear that some of these groups could be combined, for there is a relationship between planforms and axial positions such as 'sweptback', etc. Control surfaces also belong with other parts of aircraft. Proper marshalling of the terms will produce an arrangement free from 'cross division' for with facet analysis the fault is virtually impossible.

Having sorted the terms in this way, a decision must be made regarding the order in which the facets shall be arranged. Once this 'preferred order' is determined, terms derived from the facets are always cited in that order, or rather the notational elements representing the terms are so cited, in order to provide compound class numbers to stand for complex subjects.

We will concern ourselves henceforward with the first three facets listed above. It can be seen at once that the facets are named by what we called the 'characteristic' when discussing enumerative classifications formed by the process of division, and indeed with facet analysis we have discovered what the characteristic is in each case by empirically grouping families of terms and recognising the feature which they have in common, e.g. 'delta', 'rectangular', etc. are all recognised as being 'planforms' and 'planform' is therefore the characteristic of division. In classifying with a faceted classification scheme we select those elements representing the various concepts which go to make up the compound subject and synthesise them to form a compound class number. If we took the first facet above and set its terms down in a horizontal array, then took the second facet and qualified each of the existing terms with each of the terms from this new facet, and finally repeated the process with the third facet, we should be left with a classification which is exactly the same as that shown in figure 2. The end result of classification making by facet analysis is exactly the same as that from division on the classical principles, if we take all the terms produced and form an enumerative schedule in this way.

The really significant difference, apart from the fact that facet analysis relieves the classification maker of the necessity to be omniscient in order to anticipate every characteristic of division, is that a class number can be synthesised from only some of the terms available to the classifier, whereas an enumerative scheme predetermines what class numbers shall exist by the choice of the order of characteristics. If a

characteristic has been used at some high level in the heir-
archy, it cannot be ignored when we are concerned with
differences derived at a lower level, but in a faceted scheme
we are not committed to such ready-made numbers. Thus,
if we wished to classify low-wing, twin-engined military
aeroplanes, using the above classification, we could not find
a single place for the subject in the enumerative schedules as
shown in figure 2, but should have to use one or all of the
subdivisions for aeroplanes with these attributes under the
three types of aeroplanes, 'fighter', 'bomber' and 'transport',
i.e. Ac Cf Eg, Ad Cf Eg and Ae Cf Eg. With the faceted
schedules left as they are, as they are found in so-called
'faceted classifications', we do not have this problem, for we
can take the terms from the second and third facets and
ignore the first, which gives us the one place Cf Eg. Now, on
the face of it, this seems to be an undoubted advantage, and
it does facilitate the placing of a subject at a point determined
solely by the attributes which it possesses, without its being
forced unnaturally into a position depending to some extent
upon extraneous attributes. This supposed advantage is,
however, a delusion, for faceted classifications are bedevilled
by the fundamental problem of 'what you put in and what
you leave out', which is dealt with at length in chapter 4 and
which is the crux of the whole matter as far as the argument
on 'conventional' versus 'non-conventional' systems is concerned.

One other point ought to be clarified before we leave the
principles of classification. The textbooks dealing with classification as based on the classical principles are at pains to
expound the methods of Aristotelean logic, but they do not
explain the limitations of its 'genus' and 'species' principle
as far as classifications of knowledge or bibliographical classifications are concerned. This limitation is severe, because we
cannot go further than dividing a 'thing' into its 'species' or
'kinds', and are unable to introduce 'processes' or even 'parts'
of things. The statement by Phillips, which is quoted above is
left unqualified. It must be qualified to permit classification
of the kind required for classifying information. For instance,

it is impossible to provide for a class of information on 'the design of single-engined fighter aeroplanes', because this is not a 'species' of single-engined fighter aeroplanes, and 'design' is not a legitimate 'difference' for the derivation of this spurious species. Similarly, no part is a species of the whole from which it is derived. The fuselage of a fighter is not a species of fighter. It is the different kinds of fighter which are species, i.e. delta winged fighters, single-seat fighters, etc. Metcalfe contends that classifications of information need not suffer from this, because information is divided into species of information by subject, and it is information which we are classifying, not the subject of that information.[19] This seems to be begging the question, but the point is really academic anyway, because we can achieve our objective without the niceties of Aristotelean logic, and the principles of faceted classification provide one way of doing this.

There is a tendency to reject classification as something which has served its purpose well enough in the past but which has nothing to offer for the solution of current problems. It is a pity, however, that a little trouble is not taken by those who so frequently resurrect it, to understand the elementary principles concerned, for we should then be spared the sort of illustration of so-called classification which is exemplified in the proceedings of a recent American symposium.[20] Here a schedule of but ten terms is shown, with only two steps of division, but the classification maker has managed to create cross-division at both steps. The most elementary knowledge of the principles of faceted classification, or of the older logical methods would have avoided this.

We might also have a more rational system of terminology in the field of information retrieval if note were taken of some of the older principles. We have, for instance, in the United States, the reference to coding for all attributes other than the name by which a subject is known, as 'generic encoding'. The confusion which arises from this is typified by the example which Jahoda gives to demonstrate how provision can be made for 'generic searching'.[21] He cites the case of propylene, which, with hierarchical notation might be dealt with thus:

Hydrocarbon	1
Unsaturated compound	14
Mono olefin	143
C_3 Mono olefin	1435

Without hierarchical notation it would be 'generically encoded' with the descriptors 'hydrocarbon', 'mono olefin' and 'C_3 compounds'. Now if we talk of anything being generic, we must presuppose class inclusion and this implies that the classification scheme is 'enumerative' or that there is a preferred order of facets which produces this same enumerative arrangement. In many subject fields there is an obvious enumerative arrangement and classification by chemical composition is a case in point. A breakdown of the field of organic chemistry to produce 'propylene' as a species might generate the particular 'chain' shown in figure 3.

The expressions down the left-hand side of this diagram are the characteristics by which the summum genus 'Hydrocarbons' is divided. The terms in the boxes are the differences which are produced by the application of these character-

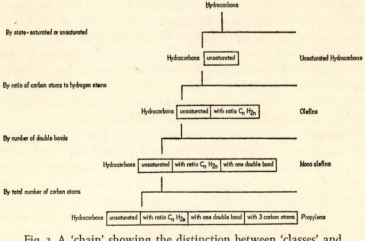

Fig 3 A 'chain' showing the distinction between 'classes' and 'differences'

istics, but only one difference per characteristic is shown as we are concerned only with that chain which produces the species 'propylene'. The terms ordinarily used to designate the compounds are listed down the right-hand side. It can be seen at once that the terms 'hydrocarbon' and 'mono olefin' are legitimate 'generic' terms in that each truly represents a class which is defined by use of all the terms which appear at that particular level and which is then subdivided into further species. The term 'with 3 carbon atoms' (i.e. C_3 compound) is not however the name of a class, but that of a difference, which occupies but one of the boxes on the final line of the diagram and which is only part of the definition of this particular class.

It might be argued that if we regard the classification as consisting of schedules of faceted terms, without presupposing a particular hierarchy it is possible to imagine many different hierarchies formed by the arrangement of the facets in different orders. It could then be said that each term would find itself representing a genus in one of such hierarchies. This argument is rather pointless, however, for acceptance of the principle would mean that every coding, except that for the term which ordinarily represents the subject, would be 'generic' coding. It is surely better to reserve the expression for those codings which represent what are generally recognised as being truly including classes as are 'hydrocarbon' and 'mono olefin'. This kind of term is the only one which has in the past, in the context of bibliographical classification, been regarded as generic and it seems to be a retrograde step to have extended its meaning to include all terms except that which specifically represents the subject being coded. The preservation of the proper meaning of the term would clarify the position, because its use is now so wide as to be virtually meaningless. It is still useful to be able to regard hierarchical notation as providing for easy generic encoding where classification is used in retrieval systems, and even the very recent newcomer to the retrieval field, the 'thesaurus' preserves the idea, at least by implication, in that its use of the principle of instructing the user to post a document to another term also when a given term is assigned admits of coding by the including class of the assigned term, but requires no action as far as other kinds of term are concerned.

In many cases the encoding which is referred to as 'generic' is coding a thing by an attribute which it possesses, by a process applied to it, etc., and whilst such coding is not just desirable, but often essential for meeting the requirements of particular retrieval systems, it should not be called by this name. A thing coded may legitimately be regarded as a species of several classes and generic encoding need not be tied to the hierarchical coding of a fixed classification scheme, but the use of the term 'generic' should be confined to those cases where there is a clear case for it. Subjects are sometimes deliberately split up into elemental terms so that a group of such terms together form a description of a subject in order to provide for retrieval by citation of one or more of the concepts when the overall subject coded is not the actual subject of search and these are commonly referred to as 'semantic factors'. This seems to be a perfectly reasonable name for such concepts and we should do better to think more often in terms of searching by 'semantic factors' rather than by 'generic codes' for we should then concern ourselves with subject specification rather than subject classification, which comes into the picture only when we make provision for retrieving information on a subject when a search is made by naming a class of which the subject can reasonably be regarded as a species.

When we have completed the making of schedules for a bibliographic classification scheme we are left with the need to provide two important auxiliary devices. The first of these is a notation, and the second is an alphabetical index to the schedules. The purpose of notation is to 'mechanise' the arranging of things classified by the schedules. The word 'mechanise' is used, not in the sense of the application of machines to do a job, but in the sense which the Shorter Oxford English Dictionary ascribes to the word 'mechanical' when it equates it with 'automatic', the relevant definition of the latter being 'not accompanied by volition or consciousness'. Once the order of terms in the schedules is determined, this order is fixed by attaching to the terms symbols which have easily recognised ordinal value, of which arabic numerals and the letters of the alphabet are the best known. When documents, or records of documents, which bear elements of the notation are handled, their arrangement is easy because of this recognised order, and finding or filing them is an 'automatic' or 'mechanical' process. The absence of notation would necessitate the reclassification of every document each time it had to be returned to the file, assuming that the documents were filed in a classified sequence.

There is an excellent illustration of the value of notation in a letter written by Thomas Jefferson to his friend James Ogilvie[22] who had been granted the use of the library at Monticello, Jefferson's home at Charlottesville:

> 'As after using a book, you may be at a loss in returning it to its exact place, and they cannot be found again when misplaced, it will be better to leave them on a table in the room. My familiarity with their places will enable me to replace them readily.'

Jefferson had arranged the books on his shelves according to a classification scheme of his own, and if after he had done this he had assigned a notation to the scheme, then the return of the books to their rightful places would have been a 'mechanical' process for Ogilvie and there would have been no need for Jefferson's fears that his orderly arrangement would be upset.

Notation is a fairly complex subject, but it is purely subordinate to the classification itself and it must meet the demands which the scheme makes on it. A classification scheme must not be modified to the slightest extent to suit the notation for notation is the servant of classification and any concessions to it may mar the quality of the scheme. Consequently the demands of a complex scheme on its notation can be very severe, for there are several different kinds of difficulty which can arise. Two of these are the limitation of the number of collateral species which can be catered for by a hierarchical notation of limited base length (the base of decimal notation is 10, i.e. the 10 digits 0–9) and the problem of interpolating new subjects both in 'chain' (i.e. vertically) and in 'array' (i.e. horizontally). An example of the former type of interpolation is that of introducing the division of aeroplanes by type of propulsion before division by number of engines, as discussed on page 32.

There is also the general problem of the desirability or otherwise of having a notation which is hierarchical, or one which is purely ordinal. The former type preserves the order of the schedules, which is the main purpose of notation, but it also reflects the hierarchy of the schedules, so that we recognise from the structure of a particular class number what other classes are subordinate to it and exactly how far we need go along the linear array of books, catalogue cards, etc., before we have exhausted the class and all its divisions. It is also apparent what other classes are collateral with it, and what is its containing class. Thus, in figure 2 we know that if we have selected the class number 3.43 that only numbers consisting of this number and additional digits will be subordinate classes, that all other numbers differing from it only in the second place after the point, i.e. 3.42, 3.44, etc., will represent collateral classes and that the class is itself a species of the class represented by 3.4.

The notation shown in the faceted arrangement on page 34 is also hierarchical in that the structure of the schedules is reflected by a synthesised class symbol such as Ac Cd Gf Je Kd—Control of delta winged single-engined fighters. Difficulty would be experienced with these particular schedules in some sections however, because, though they serve to show the process of facet analysis, they have not been completely rationalised. The terms in the facets 'Planform' and 'Position determined relative to an axis' for instance, are not entirely mutually exclusive, but this is a problem of the connotation of terms and consequent difficulty in facet analysis. There is no fault as far as the hierarchical nature of the notation goes.

With a purely ordinal notation the order of the schedules is preserved for all purposes, but no attempt is made to show hierarchy and we might, for instance, with these faceted schedules, have spread the three letters A, B, C, each subdivided by the whole of the alphabet, or as many letters as necessary, over the whole breakdown. This might have shown 'wings of fighters' as collateral with 'twin engined fighters' notationally. There is some contention that hierarchical notation is unnecessary, but it does have the advantage of delimiting the area of search on shelves and in catalogues and indexes, and if 'chain indexing' procedure is used it simplifies the process of making index entries so that much of this work can be transferred from the indexer to clerical labour.

A lengthy discourse on this complex problem of notation would be out of place here, but a simple explanation of the subject is to be found in the book by Palmer and Wells[23] and an excellent and exhaustive treatise by Coates is to be found in the Proceedings of the Dorking Conference.[24] This latter paper shows how virtually every contingency can be met, though some concessions have to be made. There is no point in arguing the case against classification on the grounds of notational problems unless these are insurmountable. The trouble is often that notation and classification are taken to be one and the same thing. On the contrary, a classification scheme must stand or fall on its merits as such. If it stands, then notation must be made to serve it properly.

In special libraries in Great Britain, where the classified catalogue has been much used, particularly that based on the Universal Decimal Classification, there has been a tendency to neglect the alphabetical index to the classified file. This seems to stem from the idea that a classified catalogue is self-sufficient and that the user should be sufficiently conversant with the classification scheme to find his way about the catalogue without reference to an index. In the nature of things, however, any comprehensive scheme, whatever its quality, can hardly be assimilated in all its ramifications by anyone, apart perhaps from a cataloguer whose sole activity is maintaining the catalogue and index. If this is admitted, it does not detract from the arguments of the protagonists of the classified catalogue that useful collocation of related subjects is brought about and that this is no less useful on account of the need for an alphabetical index to point out the location of the appropriate area of the scheme. In theory we should have the best of both worlds—specific reference through an alphabetical index, and generic survey by the proper display of related subjects.

Alphabetical indexes to classified catalogues range from the simplest affairs which cover only the broadest heads, being nothing more than, or even less than, the index to the classification schedules themselves, to elaborate structures of the 'chain index' variety. It is necessary for retrieval of specific information from classified files of moderate to great complexity to provide an index of commensurate specificity. This is not difficult if subjects are easily designated in spite of their being minute divisions of the subject field concerned, provided that such subjects are not compounds of a number of significant subject elements. An example of this type of index is that compiled for the ASLIB Cranfield Research Project, where the specific subject was taken as entry word and qualification made when necessary by quoting the immediate superordinate class or classes as far as was necessary to distinguish the various contexts of the indexed subject.[25]

For the purpose of retrieval systems for the kind of information with which we are concerned in this book, i.e. that which is 'multi-topical', only one kind of index for the classified catalogue is of real interest to us, and that is the 'chain index' developed by Ranganathan. 'Chain procedure' is a perfectly simple method and provides for entry under each of the terms of the complex subject in a rigidly controlled way. The indexing of the subject mentioned above 'Control of delta winged single-engined fighters', which would take the class symbol Ac Cd Gf Je Kd would be carried out as follows. The terms represented by the notational elements are set down in the reverse order of the class symbol, in order to provide the basic entry, and the full class symbol is cited as the relevant point at which to consult the classified file for this compound subject:

CONTROL: DELTA: WINGS:
SINGLE-ENGINED: FIGHTERS   Ac Cd Gf Je Kd

Further entries are made by progressively deleting the first term and the corresponding notational element (i.e. the last):

DELTA: WINGS: SINGLE-ENGINED: FIGHTERS	Ac Cd Gf Je
WINGS: SINGLE-ENGINED: FIGHTERS	Ac Cd Gf
SINGLE-ENGINED: FIGHTERS	Ac Cd
FIGHTERS	Ac

Thus the entry for this compound subject will be found whatever term is selected as entry word to the chain index, the theory being that all the entries in the classified file which are subordinate to that at which entry is actually made, should be searched, and the distance necessary to search down is obviously greater the broader the heading chosen for consultation of the chain index. It is apparent also, that this searching will have to be done at many different points in the classified file, for the term chosen for entry to the chain index is likely to be shown to be used in different combinations with other terms and many or all of these combinations may be relevant. A useful account of the principles of chain indexing is that by Mills.[26]

This chapter has been devoted to as brief a summary as possible of classification and its relation to the problems of documentation. The shortcomings of bibliographical classification schemes as we know them, and of other conventional methods, as far as modern information retrieval requirements are concerned, will be dealt with in chapter 4.

REFERENCES

1 Luce, A. A. *Teach yourself logic*, EUP, London, 1958, p. 83.

2 Stebbing, L. S. *A modern elementary logic*, 5th edition, Methuen, London, 1952, pp. 24-6.

3 Cohen, M. R. and Nagel, E. *An introduction to logic* (paperback edition of the first part of *An introduction to logic and scientific method*, 1934), Routledge, London, 1963, p. 123.

4   Lee, H. N. *Symbolic logic: an introductory textbook for non-mathematicians*, Routledge, London, 1962, pp. 62-91.

5   Wolf, A. *Textbook of logic*, 2nd edition, Allen and Unwin, London, 1938, p. 172.

6   Metcalfe, J. *Information indexing and subject cataloguing: alphabetical: classified: co-ordinate: mechanical*, Scarecrow Press, New York, 1957, p. 297.

7   Wright, W. E. The subject approach to knowledge: historical aspects and purposes. In *The subject analysis of library materials*, edited by M. F. Tauber, School of Library Service, Columbia University, New York, 1953, p. 10.

8   Chapman, V. J. *The algae*, Macmillan, London, 1962.

9   Classification: an interdisciplinary problem. Proceedings of an ASLIB Conference, London, 6th April 1962. *ASLIB Proceedings*, Vol. 14, No. 8, August 1962, pp. 222-62.

10 Richardson, E. C. *Classification, theoretical and practical*, 3rd edition, H. W. Wilson, New York, 1930.

11 Hulme, E. W. The principles of book classification. *Library Association Record*, Vol. 13, 1911, pp. 354-8, 389-94, 444-9; Vol. 14, 1912, pp. 39-46, 174-81, 216-21. (Association of Assistant Librarians, Reprint No. 1, London, 1950).

12 Bliss, H. E. *A bibliographic classification*, 4 vols., H. W. Wilson, New York, 1940-53.

13 Cutter, C. A. *Expansive classification*, Boston, 1891-3.

14 Ranganathan, S. R. *Elements of library classification*, edited by B. I. Palmer, 2nd edition, Association of Assistant Librarians, London, 1959, p. 2.

15 Phillips, W. H. *A primer of book classification*, 5th edition, Association of Assistant Librarians, London, 1961.

16 Sayers, W. C. B. *An introduction to library classification*, 9th edition, Grafton, London, 1954.

17 ——. *A manual of classification for librarians and bibliographers*, 3rd edition, Grafton, London, 1955.

18 Phillips, op. cit., p. 13.

19 Metcalfe, op. cit., pp. 30-1.

20 Holm, B. E. The information problem in industry. In *Proceedings of the EJC engineering information symposium*, 17th January 1962. Engineers Joint Council, New York, 1962, p. 10, Fig. 6.

21 Jahoda, G. *Correlative indexing systems for the control of research records*. Columbia University, D.L.S. thesis, 1960. University Microfilms. Mic 60-3082, p. 47.

22 Jefferson, Thomas. Letter to James Ogilvie, dated Washington, January 31st 1806.

23 Palmer, B. I. and Wells, A. J. *The fundamentals of library classification*, Allen and Unwin, London, 1951, pp. 60-75.

24 Coates, E. J. Notation in classification. In *Proceedings of the International Study Conference on Classification for Information Retrieval* held at Dorking 13th–17th May 1957. ASLIB, London, 1957, pp. 51-64.

25 ASLIB Cranfield Research Project. *Alphabetical Index for the Universal Decimal Classification*, Cranfield, 1960.

26 Mills, J. Chain indexing and the classified catalogue. *Library Association Record*, Vol. 57, No. 4, April 1955, pp. 141-8.

3

The Alphabetical
Subject Catalogue

The alphabetical subject catalogue is based on the principle of subject specification rather than subject classification. Subject headings, which are filed in the universally-known alphabetical order, are formulated according to rules which determine the degree to which vocabulary is controlled. This in turn determines the degree to which coincidence in subject specification is achieved between indexer and searcher and consequently the capability of the catalogue to retrieve efficiently. Though classification need not be consciously considered in the compilation of such catalogues, the subject relationships which a classification displays by collocation, and which are not evident from the order of entries in the alphabetical subject catalogue, are usually shown by the use of appropriate references. There is some difference of opinion as to what constitutes a catalogue as against an index, but for the purpose of this discussion the two are taken to be synonymous because the problems of subject headings in this context are common to both.

Two distinct types of alphabetical subject catalogue are recognised: the alphabetico-specific and the alphabetico-classed. The former uses entries under headings which consist solely of the names of the specific subjects of documents, arrangement being alphabetical by those specific names. The headings in the alphabetico-classed catalogue consist of the names of specific subjects subordinated to the names of super-ordinate classes. Arrangement of headings is again strictly alphabetical so that though hierarchies are shown, collocation of entries depends partly on classification, partly on the accidental spelling of terms. The relevant hierarchies extend to that level which is considered appropriate to the purpose of the particular catalogue. As an example of the kinds of heading used, the entry for the subject 'Bombers' in an alphabetico-specific catalogue for a general collection of documents would appear simply as:

BOMBERS

If the catalogue were of the alphabetico-classed variety the heading might appear thus:

AIRCRAFT—HEAVIER-THAN-AIR AIRCRAFT—
AEROPLANES—MILITARY AEROPLANES—
BOMBERS

Though headings which properly belong to the alphabetico-classed type of catalogue can be found in some current catalogues and indexes, alphabetico-classed catalogues are now comparatively rare.

We ought here to consider what we mean by the word 'specific', for the sense in which it is used in the expression 'alphabetico-specific' is not the same as that implied in other contexts. For the purpose of this book 'specific' is taken to mean that a subject designation when so described, be it a class number, an alphabetical subject heading, a compounding of uniterms, descriptors, etc., is co-extensive with the subject which it represents. In other words it describes the subject completely and exactly, no matter how complex, and is not confined to citing some parts only of the compound subject, or to a broader heading than the subject as represented in a recognised hierarchy.

The word is, of course, derived from the word 'species', but this is not to say that its use must be confined to describing a thing solely on the basis of its relation to a given genus. One of the definitions of the word 'specific' given by the Shorter Oxford English Dictionary is 'Exactly named or indicated; precise, particular', and, as discussed in the last chapter, it is not always possible to describe a concept precisely by a genus-species breakdown governed strictly by logical principles. The introduction of a process term to a hierarchy for substantives at once breaks the rules and is an example of the limitations of Aristotelean logic for this purpose. The subject designation 'Control of delta wings' may be quite specific in that it describes exactly this subject, but it is not specific in the genus-species sense for though 'delta wings' is a species of 'wings', 'control of delta wings' is not a species of 'delta wings'.

Assuming the definition of 'specific' chosen for our purpose here, an 'alphabetico-specific' heading is not necessarily any more specific than a heading used in the alphabetico-classed catalogue. The example given above for 'bombers' shows that there is no difference in specificity in the two types of catalogue, for it is explicitly stated in each case that the subject is 'bombers'. What is different is that in one case entry is made directly under the term and in the other the term is subsumed to the terms representing a chain of including classes. Haykin said 'Headings for a given topic in an alphabetico-classed and a dictionary catalog are equally specific. The difference lies in the fact that in the former the specific topic is the last element in a complex heading whereas in the latter it is named directly.'[1] It seems, therefore, that a much better name for the alphabetico-specific catalogue would be 'alphabetico-direct', for entry can be just as specific in the sense accepted here in the one type of catalogue as in the other. A useful distinction which carries this philosophy still further has been made for the purposes of the ASLIB Cranfield Research Project, where the co-extensiveness of subject designation with the subject is considered to be determined by a combination of 'specificity' and 'exhaustivity'.[2] The definition given above, will, however, serve for the purposes of discussion here.

The first to introduce any significant degree of control into alphabetical subject cataloguing was Charles Ammi Cutter, whose 'Rules for a dictionary catalog'[3] appeared in 1876. Current subject cataloguing practice still owes much to his principles. The next important step was the publication of Kaiser's book[4] in 1911. Kaiser did not have a great deal of direct influence, and though the widespread use of the 'THING –Process' breakdown in so many subject catalogues cannot be attributed directly to its advocation by him, it says a great deal for his insight into the problem.

Since Cutter and Kaiser there has not been any radical change in the basic principles on which alphabetical subject catalogues are based. Good practice has been largely dependent on the following of recognised authorities by the use of subject headings lists issued by such authorities. The best known of these in the general field are those of the Library of Congress[5] and Sears.[6] Specialised lists have been compiled for particular subject fields and the Special Libraries Association have published several such lists in the United States. It is not surprising that most of such lists have emanated from America, for the alphabetical subject catalogue has enjoyed great popularity there at the expense of the classified catalogue, whilst the reverse has been the case in Great Britain. As far as teaching the subject is concerned, the best known textbook in America is that by Mann[7] and in Great Britain that by Sharp.[8]

A very significant event in recent years was the appearance of the book by Coates,[9] whose experience as Chief Subject Cataloguer for the British National Bibliography has produced a work which is unique and which examines the problem of the form of heading and the overall structure of the alphabetical subject catalogue on a much more scientific basis than has hitherto been used. For the older and comparatively arbitrary methods of choosing headings, using principles such as those of 'usage', Coates has tried to substitute a system of determining component order in complex headings by considering how things, materials, actions, etc., are related in subject statements and formulating rules which determine order by the functions which such analysis reveals. Though Coates may have suggested only a partial solution to the problems of alphabetical subject cataloguing and detected only some of the kinds of complex subject designation which may be met, he has undoubtedly made an invaluable contribution and puts forward ideas which can be incorporated in practical cataloguing. His ideas can be recognised in the nature of the headings of the recently launched British Technology Index, of which Coates is editor.

We must now consider what we try to do when we formulate subject headings and how we endeavour to provide an overall structure for the alphabetical subject catalogue. The purpose of the rules and subject headings lists which have been compiled for use in constructing such catalogues has been to regularise the choice of heading and to ensure proper linking of chosen headings by the use of references. The former is a question of subject specification, the standardisation of which is essential for ensuring that both indexer and searcher will cite subjects in the same way. The purpose of the latter is to restore to the alphabetical subject catalogue those features which the classified catalogue is supposed to have, i.e. the display of relations between subjects, which it has lost by being arranged in alphabetical order of its headings.

As far as the formulation of headings for individual entries is concerned, it is obvious that the choice of entry word, that is the word which the searcher will select as being likely to be the first word in the heading, is of paramount importance as this will determine the point at which he chooses to make access to the catalogue. Two factors enter into this choice. The first is the question of synonymity, which is easily catered for by the choice of one term to serve for all synonyms, with reference from all the unused terms. The other is the question of component order, where a decision has to be made which will determine which of several words becomes entry word. The classic example of this is the question of the inversion or non-inversion of adjectival phrases. Should we use:

ELECTRIC MOTORS	or
MOTORS, ELECTRIC	
DE-ICING EQUIPMENT	or
EQUIPMENT, DE-ICING	
LANDING SPEED	or
SPEED, LANDING	

Coates has done excellent work in resolving problems such as this and has isolated twenty categories of types of phrase, with positive decisions on the order in which the components should be cited. This is a great improvement on the older, more nebulous rules such as Cutter's instruction to enter a compound subject under its first word, inverting only when another word in the group of words is 'decidedly' more significant.

Supposing that we have solutions to the kinds of problem outlined above, let us consider how helpful is the consistency which is thus brought about. A very significant aspect of this question, and one which seldom if ever seems to be brought into the open is this: when a decision has been made on which word is to be entry word (or 'approach term' as Coates calls it) what is the function of the terms which comprise the remainder of the heading? This is very important, for the whole philosophy of subject heading formulation is concerned with the formalisation of language for this particular purpose, and we should ask ourselves why we go to all this trouble. There are, in fact two quite distinct functions which can be performed by this part of a heading:

1 It can be regarded, together with the entry word, as being a brief indicative abstract of the subject of the document. The heading is then used as just that, so that when it is encountered by the searcher as a result of his approach through the entry word he can accept or reject the document which the entry represents according to whether it is relevant to his requirements or not.

2 The formalisation of subject heading language is such that the heading is not only a satisfactory summary of the subject of the document, but the heading's construction depends on such definite rules that the searcher can match exactly, or nearly exactly, the heading chosen by the indexer, and can therefore consult a more precise point in the catalogue than if he concerned himself solely with the entry word for access. This is obviously highly significant if a large number of entries appear under a given entry term, for a great deal of 'sorting through' or 'sequential scanning' is thus eliminated.

The indexes to 'Chemical Abstracts' are of the first type, for it is often, if not usually the case that all the entries under a given entry word have to be scanned in order to determine which, if any, will be relevant to a search. Some attempt is made to collocate entries which take the same form such as:

SULPHUR   effect on bases in soils
              benzoic acid formation from toluene
              on metallized C catalysts
              bioassay dip test for insecticides
          formation of, from Bu nitrate and NaSH
              from CaS_5
              from C and H_2S
              from chlorination of Cu_2S
          reaction of, with aluminate and silicate melts
              with amines

This is often very helpful and does save a great deal of searching, for if a search is satisfactorily concluded by consulting such a group of entries and no more, it is obvious that searching is done more economically. Nevertheless, it must be said that searching in these indexes and particularly in the decennial indexes, whose excellent quality is not surpassed by any other indexing done on a similar scale, can be laborious. If the very difficult, and perhaps impossible, problem of providing headings of the second type could be solved, searching should be less time-consuming.

Some catalogues and indexes, particularly those of particular collections do attempt to provide headings of the second type, and indeed the headings of Congress and Sears' List succeed to a large extent in providing for more precise location than mere entry words give. But these are tools for broad fields and it is comparatively easy to provide for use of terms subsequent to the entry term as significant filing terms, because it is that easy to provide and recognise mutually exclusive sub-headings. 'Chemical Abstracts' has a much more serious problem because of the nature of its field.

If, after having chosen the correct entry term, we are content to regard headings of the first type as meeting our

requirements, is it worth while to go to the trouble of formalising the whole of a heading for the sole purpose of stating
what a document is about, so that its relevance or irrelevance
can be determined? If we must check every entry under the
entry word, would not any kind of statement subsumed to the
entry word, given the usual requirements of brevity, clarity,
etc., serve just as well? There is little doubt that the answer
must be in the affirmative, and indeed if the wording of the
heading is determined solely by considering the way in which
the subject can best be expressed, the heading may serve this
particular purpose better for not being tied to unnecessary
formalisation.

Everything points however, to the need for qualification of
the entry word in a way which reduces sequential scanning
to a minimum. (Indeed if this is not the case, there cannot,
as discussed in chapter 4, be justification for using 'co-ordinate'
systems.) As far as alphabetical catalogues and indexes of the
conventional, visible type are concerned it is only formalisation of headings which will help in reducing the area of search
by locating the entry point more precisely. It is implicit in
this that the principles and rules of formulation of headings
must be understood by both indexer and searcher so that
precise and consistent specification is always achieved by both.

Now it is paradoxical that it is this very principle which
has been the root cause of much of the uninformed criticism
which has been levelled at what can be regarded as the best
general subject index published to date, if the criteria are
consistency of the form of headings and the rationality of
overall structure. This, the British Technology Index, edited
by E. J. Coates, began publication in January 1962 and it is
unfortunate that no explanation of the way in which its
headings are formulated appeared until the publication of the
first annual volume in July 1963. This is not to say that the
information was not available, for Coates' book, published in
1960, expounded the principles on which the BTI's structure
is clearly based and the critics might have been less voluble
had they taken the trouble to try to discover the principles
on which Coates was working.

Even now, the introduction to the first annual volume of BTI does not explain everything, and this is not surprising because of the very great difficulty of formulating simple, and at the same time all-embracing rules. It is not easy to see, for instance why there should be the apparent inconsistency between the two headings shown below, and it is understandable that the uninitiated, and even those who have read the explanation in the annual volume, should regard this as a sign of inconsistency rather than of quality:

MOTOR VEHICLES, Engines, Valves, Poppet
MOTOR VEHICLES, Engines, Exhaust Valves

The searcher may well wonder why the expression 'exhaust valves' is entered as it stands, while 'poppet valves' is entered as 'valves, poppet'. The formulation of these sub-headings involves two of the categories cited by Coates. First, 'poppet valves' belongs to the category 'Thing distinguished by citation of Principle of Action' and Coates has determined that the order for this type of phrase shall be THING, Action. The thing here is 'valve' and the principle of action is the 'poppet' principle. The form of heading is therefore 'Valves, Poppet'. In the case of 'Exhaust valves' the relevant category is 'Thing serving or instrumental to Action'. Here the action served by the valve is the process of 'exhausting' and as component order for the category is ACTION, Thing, we have the form 'Exhaust valves'.

Coates has gone to a great deal of trouble to try to achieve this situation wherein the form which a heading is to take is clear, on the grounds of the nature of its component parts. He has succeeded in formulating some rules where virtually none existed before and the penalty has been a considerable amount of hostility. There has also been criticism on the grounds that the philosophy behind these newer techniques is bound up with classification and it is certainly the case that Coates believes that classificatory principles can usefully be applied to alphabetical subject cataloguing, particularly with regard to the construction of a proper structure of genus-species and collateral references. It is equally certain that the kinds of relationship which Coates has tabulated for the purpose of the formulation of individual headings can be applied without the slightest reference to classification, and the cataloguer or indexer who chooses to take advantage of them is still at liberty to build up the reference structure of the index on the customary basis of his personal judgement.

The kind of referencing referred to here is of course the 'see also' network between related subjects. The BTI also references very thoroughly from forms of headings not used, i.e. those of non-standard component order, to those which are and this 'see' reference structure is again not concerned in any way with classification. It might be argued that such elaborate referencing is unnecessary if the basic intention of standardising headings is successfully carried out and strictly speaking this argument is valid. It is quite clear, however, that it is not all users of the index who understand its structure, or trouble to try to understand it, and even for these the BTI is a very reliable tool on account of its providing for guidance regardless of what component of a heading may be first consulted. The trouble is, of course, that with a thorough reference structure for complex headings, references can be so numerous that the system becomes unwieldy because of their sheer weight. Undoubtedly many such references could be eliminated if it could be assumed that the searcher had a knowledge of the way in which headings are compiled, for consultation of headings which are known not to be used would not occur. In other words, for efficient catalogue use, the only system is one in which the indexer and the searcher know the rules. Even when this ideal situation does not exist, as is the case with BTI, the application of such rules by the indexers must make for greater efficiency in index compilation.

The two examples of Coates' rules given above demonstrate the nature of their author's approach to the problems and the fact that these particular examples happen to produce what is apparently an incongruous pattern should not be taken to be an argument against the soundness of the rules. They were cited in order to demonstrate what the reaction of the user of such an index who is not familiar with the principle involved might be. Coates' rules as a whole may prove to be quite acceptable, but what seems doubtful is whether a really significant proportion of all the possible problems has really been catered for.

We might ask ourselves, in this connection, why it has been necessary in the past to have both rules for the compilation of alphabetical subject catalogues and subject headings lists. Surely, if the rules are adequate then all purposes should be served as the application of such rules should produce automatically a satisfactory pattern of headings for the catalogue. The answer to this is probably that the complexity of the problem of the formation of headings is such that it is impossible to determine an acceptably small number of rules and that in the final analysis a rule is made for virtually every heading which arises in practical work. A rule is then not so much a rule as a more or less arbitrary decision by the cataloguer as to what form a heading shall take, and this decision is then recorded not as a rule but as the actual subject heading chosen. The final result of this, is of course, a subject headings list and this can be regarded as the manifestation of a set of rules, perhaps one for every heading, though the rules are not explicitly, or even implicitly stated by the resulting list. Indeed the compiler of such a list is absolved from the responsibility of even thinking in terms of rules.

Most of the subject headings lists which have been published have provided for headings which can only be regarded, by special library standards, as very broad. The special librarian or information officer who can take a list compiled for some collection other than his own is fortunate indeed. Such lists seldom go beyond provision for a main heading, comprising perhaps a substantive, with one or two adjectival qualifications and provision for a single subheading to be used with it. A typical example might be:

WINGS, SWEPTBACK, SUPERSONIC—Stability, Longitudinal

This is patently inadequate for subjects of even moderate complexity, but the important thing is that the form of the heading is easily recognised and no great effort is needed on the part of the catalogue user to familiarise himself with such formalisation to an extent which will enable him to match with a fair degree of certainty the heading chosen by the indexer. On the assumption that formalisation is essential in order to reduce sorting through large numbers of entries under a given entry word, it is obvious that what is required is an extension of the principles which produce such headings as that cited above, in order to give the same recognisable construction but with provision for stating more complex subjects.

The heading cited above is typical of the very large number of headings which cover subjects described by the citation of processes, properties, problems, etc., applied to substantives. If such headings are extended to cover more complex subjects it is usually necessary to introduce new types of relationship, and it is probable that it is the formidable nature of this problem which has tended to restrict such development. It is, however, possible to secure some extension, with the preservation of control, by using what might be called 'relational terms' to link two or more headings of the 'Thing–process' type. Metcalfe touches briefly on this type of term, which he calls an 'intermediate subheading'[10] but he is concerned with the philosophy of classification brought about by the introduction of such terms, not with facilitating more specific headings, and he gives little guidance on how they should be used.

It is undoubtedly possible, in some fields at least, to introduce such terms and to achieve greater specificity and this has been done successfully in a catalogue of a small collection of research reports in the field of man-made fibres. It is obvious that such a catalogue can be manageable only if the number of relational terms is restricted and it so happened that experience in this field showed that the vast majority of subjects could be catered for by a very small number of such terms. The residue of cases for which the accepted relational terms were not suitable, would have required a disproportionate number of additional terms, the applicability of each of which would have been limited, but this residue was comparatively small and the limitation of the schedule of terms to those of wide and general application preserved good control without too much loss in the facility for specific subject designation.

The relational terms were found in most cases to fall into pairs, one term of each pair being the reciprocal of its partner. The terms used were as follows:

> Applications ⎫
> Using   ⎭
> Causing   ⎫
> Caused by   ⎭
> Affecting   ⎫
> Affected by ⎭
> Compared with
> Synchronisation with
> Reactions with

Examples of the uses of these terms are as follows:

THREADLINES—Friction—Affected by—SPINNING FINISH —Viscosity

SPINNING FINISH—Viscosity—Affecting—THREADLINES— Friction

LIGHTS, ARC, XENON—Applications—YARNS—Degradation, Light—Testing

YARNS—Degradation, Light—Testing—Using—LIGHTS, ARC, XENON

PACKS—Blockage—Caused by—NYLON 6.6—Gelation

NYLON 6.6—Gelation—Causing—PACKS—Blockage

It will be seen that these headings are simply a compounding of headings of the usual 'Thing–Process', 'Thing–Property', etc., type and that pairs of reciprocal terms enable entry to be made under both of such linked headings. The terms which are not paired provide the same facility of course, as the relationships are reversible: A compared with B is the same as B compared with A. It has been the practice in this catalogue to provide entry under both parts of the heading automatically, with very few exceptions. In order to avoid too much complexity no more than one relational term has been permitted in one heading. Where the substantive is common to both of the linked parts it is dropped from the second part:

> NYLON 6.6—Oxidation, Thermal—Affected by—
> Drawtwisting
> NYLON 6.6—Drawtwisting—Affecting—Oxidation,
> Thermal

not:

> NYLON 6.6—Oxidation, Thermal—Affected by—
> NYLON 6.6—Drawtwisting
> etc.

This reversing of headings is one of the techniques used in this catalogue to provide for access by every likely approach term, but it caters for substantives only, and not for subheadings. It is not usual in alphabetical subject catalogues to indicate to the searcher every place where a subheading has been used, but this has been done in this catalogue. The lack of such provision can be justified only on the grounds that a particular process, etc. is of interest to the searcher in a particular context only and there may be such grounds in a general catalogue. In a special collection, however, a process is often, if not usually, of interest as a technique in its own right, regardless of particular applications. Thus the process of 'crimping' in the textile fibres field is common to many types of yarn and entries may appear in a catalogue for:

> YARNS, CARPET—Crimping
> YARNS, HEAVY DENIER—Crimping
> YARNS, KNITTING, WARP—Crimping
> YARNS, TYRE CORD—Crimping

The searcher requiring all available information on crimping is likely to be interested in most if not all of the documents represented by these headings and the usual practice is to leave it to him to think of all the terms to which the subheading 'Crimping' may be subsumed. Such subheadings are what are referred to as 'distributed relatives' when discussed in relation to chain indexing and relative indexing for the classified catalogue. Indeed, the main purpose of such indexing is to gather these terms together at one point and to indicate where they have been used in the classified file or where they appear in the schedules of the classification scheme.

There has been no limitation placed on the number of subheadings used with a main heading, provided that a proper order of 'dependence' is evident in the arrangement. Thus in the heading, NYLON 6.6—Crystallisation—Rates—Measuring, the existence of each of the component terms is dependent on its predecessors. The absence of 'Crystallisation' would make nonsense of 'Rates—Measuring', as would the absence of 'Rates' make 'Measuring' meaningless. The procedure for indicating the places when subheadings, subsubheadings, etc., have been used is as follows. New headings are formed, by deleting one term at a time from the beginning of the basic heading and reference is made from each such new heading to the basic heading, using the expression 'used with'. Thus for the basic heading, THREADLINES—Tension—Compensating devices, the following references would be made:

> Tension—Compensating devices
> *used with*
> THREADLINES
>
> Compensating devices
> *used with*
> THREADLINES—Tension

Some of the references produced by this method provide for reference from terms which are not likely to be sought and these can be suppressed at the discretion of the indexer. One advantage of this system as against chain indexing is that all the terms appear in natural language in every entry and reference, and the searcher is not left to consult another file or part of a file to see the context.

For the purpose of handling references of this kind, the

parts of compound headings linked by relational terms are regarded as independent and referencing carried only to the end of each part. No provision of this kind is made to show where relational terms themselves are used. They are regarded always as unsought.

References of the usual 'see' variety are made from the unused to the used form of adjectival phrases, etc. The full set of entries and references for a document on 'the effect of take-off tension from conical containers on variation in leg length of stockings' would appear as follows:

CONTAINERS, CONICAL—Take-off—Tension—Affecting—LEGS (STOCKINGS)—Length—Variation

LEGS (STOCKINGS)—Length—Variation—Affected by—CONTAINERS, CONICAL—Take-off—Tension

> Take-off—Tension
> *used with*
> CONTAINERS, CONICAL
>
> Tension
> *used with*
> CONTAINERS, CONICAL—Take-off
>
> Length—Variation
> *used with*
> LEGS (STOCKINGS)
>
> Variation
> *used with*
> LEGS (STOCKINGS)—Length
>
> CONICAL CONTAINERS
> *see*
> CONTAINERS, CONICAL
>
> STOCKINGS, LEGS
> *see*
> LEGS (STOCKINGS)

The procedures outlined above are peculiar to this particular catalogue, but the problems usually met with in alphabetical subject cataloguing work have, of course, been encountered. Much trouble has been avoided by following Coates' rules to a large extent, with the notable exception of the entry of parts of things directly under their names with parenthetical qualification by the name of the whole, rather than under the name of the whole, as advocated by Coates. It was also felt that the use of the hyphen between main headings and subheadings and between individual subheadings, with the use of the comma reserved for use in inverted adjectival phrases was better than the almost universal use of the comma as in the British Technology Index.

Compilation of a catalogue on these lines is a fairly laborious business and it is necessary to maintain elaborate records of the uses of terms in a file other than the catalogue proper in order to ensure consistency and overall control. Nevertheless, if the documents are of vital importance the work may be justified if much of the reference to the catalogue is made by library users who prefer the direct approach provided by such a catalogue to the mechanics of a system based on optical stencil cards, needle sorted cards, etc.

The foregoing has been concerned with the formulation of headings for the alphabetico-specific catalogue, and not with the structure of references between such headings, except insofar as these come into the description of the particular catalogue described. The question of references is an important one, for it is by the use of a reference structure that the alphabetical catalogue compensates for the lack of grouping of related subjects as found in the classified catalogue. The general practice has for a very long time been to refer down from containing classes to subordinate classes and across between collateral classes, but not upwards from subordinate classes to superordinate classes. Here we are, of course talking of 'see also' references whose purpose is to suggest to the searcher that as he is interested in the subject whose name he has turned up in the catalogue, he may also be interested in the other subject or subjects referred to. Thus, if he turns up PNEUMATIC MACHINERY he may be helped by the reference.

PNEUMATIC MACHINERY
see also
COMPRESSORS
TURBINES

If he turns up COMPRESSORS the reference

COMPRESSORS
see also
TURBINES

may be of help. Reference is not usually made upwards though the arguments against the practice have not been very convincing. Haykin sums up the case thus: 'References from the specific to the broader heading would have the effect of sending the reader on a wild goose chase . . . furthermore, if references from all topics comprehended within a given subject were to be made, on the assumption that the reader would find in treatises on that subject material on these topics, the catalogue would be cluttered up with a plethora of references.'[11] In recent years, however, there has been a shift in attitude and it is now held by some, and particularly by Coates,[12] that references should be made up as well as down. Coates' argument is that searching in a catalogue or on shelves takes the course of specific to generic when a classified arrangement exists and that the same channels ought to be signposted for the searcher in the alphabetical subject catalogue. Coates also argues that the reference structure of the catalogue should be based on a classification scheme,[9, 12] but in a 'Tentative Code of Rules for Alphabetico-Specific Entry' Metcalfe includes a rule which states 'Do not use subject classification or class numbers to determine references'.[13]

The references discussed above are of the 'see also' variety, i.e. those which suggest to the reader other terms under which pertinent material may be found. These must be distinguished from 'see' references which are instructions found under a term which is not used at all to consult a term which is used in its stead, i.e. its synonym or near-synonym. The expression 'reference' and more particularly 'cross-reference' is often

c

used, quite wrongly for 'added entry'. Ideally, when a document covers several different subjects, entry should be made under each subject, that is the bibliographical details should be found under each heading. The searcher is then never referred from one of the several entries used to represent the document to another. This is 'multiple entry', not cross-reference and it should always be so called. In the interests of economy of space multiple entry must sometimes be rejected, particularly in printed catalogues and indexes, and the practice is then to make entry under the main subject of a document and to refer from the subsidiary subject to the name of the main subject. Thus, we have in the 1961 volume of Engineering Index a reference, BICYCLE MANUFACTURE see METALS FINISHING, because under METALS FINISHING there appears an article on temperature and rate of heating for lacquering and vitreous enamelling which deals with the finishing of several articles, including bicycle frames. This is, of course, a different type of 'see' reference from that which caters only for synonyms and which is the only type which should be found in the pure alphabetico-specific catalogue with multiple entry.

There is still much to be said for the alphabetical subject catalogue on account of ease of use and general simplicity. It should not be rejected on the assumption that because it is conventional it is inadequate. The factors to be considered in judging the need or otherwise for non-conventional systems in particular situations will be dealt with in the next chapter.

REFERENCES

1   Haykin, D. J. *Subject headings: a practical guide,* Government Printing Office, Washington, 1951, p. 3.
2   Mills, J. ASLIB Cranfield Research Project. One-day Conference, London, 5th February 1963. Unpublished notes for paper by Mr Jack Mills (since published as C. W. Cleverdon and J. Mills, The testing of index language devices, *ASLIB Proceedings,* Vol. 15, No. 4, April 1963, pp. 106-30).

3   Cutter, C. A. *Rules for a dictionary catalogue*, 4th edition, Government Printing Office, Washington, 1904. Republished by the Library Association, London, 1948.

4   Kaiser, J. *Systematic indexing*, London, 1911.

5   Library of Congress, *Subject headings used in the dictionary catalogs of Library of Congress*, edited by Marguerite V. Quattlebaum, Washington, 1957.

6   Sears, M. E. *List of subject headings*, 6th edition by B. M. Frick, H. W. Wilson, New York, 1950.

7   Mann, M. *Introduction to cataloguing and the classification of books*, 2nd edition, American Library Association, Chicago, 1943.

8   Sharp, H. A. *Cataloguing: a textbook for use in libraries*, 4th edition with an introduction by L. S. Jast, Grafton, London, 1948.

9   Coates, E. J. *Subject catalogues: headings and structure*, Library Association, London, 1960.

10 Metcalfe, J. *Information indexing and subject cataloguing: alphabetical: classified: co-ordinate: mechanical*, Scarecrow Press, New York, 1957, p. 238.

11 Haykin, D. J. Subject headings: principles and development. In *The subject analysis of library materials*, edited by M. F. Tauber, School of Library Service, Columbia University, New York, 1953, p. 51.

12 Coates, E. J. The use of BNB in dictionary cataloguing. *Library Association Record*, Vol. 59, No. 6, June 1957, pp. 197-202.

13 Metcalfe, J. *Subject classifying and indexing of libraries and literature*, Scarecrow Press, New York, 1959, p. 291.

4

The Shortcomings
of Conventional Systems

The last two chapters have discussed the practical manifestations of the two principles which we have available to us as
bases for information storage and retrieval systems: subject
classification which attempts to arrange information into
patterns in such a way that we can recognise areas relevant
to particular subject interests, and subject specification which
attempts to designate information in such a way that designation by searcher is the same as that by indexer so that a match
can be made by locating items with that designation, without
regard to the order in which the file is stored, and in particular
without regard to an order based on classification. Whichever
principle is chosen as the basis for a particular system, success
of the system presupposes that the principle is a workable
proposition. How far is our assumption that these principles
are valid justified, as far as our application of them in conventional systems is concerned? Let us first examine classification
from this point of view.

Ideally the classification of a subject field should be such
that the users of literature in that field should readily recognise the arrangement, so that the area relevant to a particular
interest can be easily detected. This implies that the number
of possible arrangements of the subjects in the field should at
best be only one and at worst a very small number. Nevertheless, a classification scheme whose arrangement is not
apparent, and which must be bolstered up with an elaborate
alphabetical subject index can be a useful basis for a retrieval
system, provided that the arrangement is that which caters

for the majority of demands made on the system. If the system is going to meet the one criterion which justifies bibliographical schemes, that is the proper juxtaposition of related subjects, this preferred arrangement must be clearly superior to any other. In general classification schemes, though the perfect arrangement may not have been found, the comparative broadness of subjects covered, with fairly obvious hierarchical structure, has enabled useful arrangements to be made with considerable success in application to general collections.

The attempts to develop classification schemes for special subject fields have, however, run into the difficulty caused by encountering situations wherein very large numbers of alternative groupings may be required to meet varying requirements, and a single arrangement is patently inadequate. The significant factor in considering the chances of meeting with success in applying a classification scheme is the number of alternative arrangements which are possible, for once we have determined on one arrangement, we have deprived ourselves of the possibility of using any other. Shera recognises this when he states: 'Thus the classifier is compelled to select a single relationship from all the possible relationships which any given title might have to its fellows, and to disregard the remainder, however important these may be to the users of the collection.'[1]

Let us consider the magnitude of this number of alternative arrangements. This is the same thing as considering the number of possible hierarchies, for this determines the number of ways in which all the classes in a scheme can be arranged relative to one another, and the factors which govern the number of possible hierarchies are the number of characteristics used and the number of differences produced by each characteristic.

Suppose that we have a simple classification of the kind shown in figure 2 of chapter 2, where we have divided military aeroplanes by three characteristics, each characteristic generating three differences. We will repeat the structure of the tree here, designating the differences with capital letters for the first characteristic, arabic numerals for the second, and lower case letters for the third:

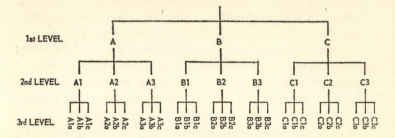

Considering the 1st level in this diagram, we can set down the differences derived by the first characteristic in any order we choose and as we have 3 differences A, B and C, the number of possible orders available to us is 3! (factorial 3, i.e. $3 \times 2 \times 1$). Considering the 2nd level we have 3 arrays, each comprising three new classes derived by the addition of the new differences 1, 2 and 3. Each of these arrays can have its classes arranged in 3! orders and as we have 3 arrays the number of ways of arranging all the classes at this level is $3! \times 3! \times 3! = (3!)^3$ (N.B. *not* 9!). The total number of hierarchies possible down to this level is the number possible at level 1 multiplied by the number possible at level 2 = $3! \times (3!)^3$. The number of possible orders of classes at the 3rd level is again the number of possible orders within each array to the power of the number of arrays, which is $(3!)^9$, so that the number of possible hierarchies down to level 3 is $3! \times (3!)^3 \times (3!)^9$.

This number of hierarchies does not take into account the fact that we could have introduced our characteristics in a different order, i.e. we could have divided first by applying differences 1, 2 and 3, instead of A, B and C. It is evident that the introduction of this additional facility for altering the order of things in 'chain' (i.e. downwards), in addition to altering the order in 'array' (i.e. across), increases the number of possible hierarchies still further. As the number of characteristics is 3, the numbers of orders in which they can be applied is 3! and we must therefore multiply our original number by this figure. The total number of hierarchies which can be formed to classify things by using 3 characteristics, each generating 3 differences is therefore:

$$3! \times 3! \times (3!)^3 \times (3!)^9$$

For the general case, the number of hierarchies which can be formed to classify things by using x characteristics, each generating x differences is:

$$x! \times x! \times (x!)^x \times (x!)^{x^2} \times (x!)^{x^3} \ldots \times (x!)^{x^{(x-1)}}$$

This formula produces a phenomenally high number, even for our case of only 3 characteristics with 3 differences each. It is likely, however, that once we have decided at a given level what the order of the differences newly introduced will be, we shall apply them in that order in each array. In other words, in our example above, at the 2nd level, when we introduce differences, 1, 2 and 3, if we apply them in that order under A, then we shall almost certainly apply them in that order under B and C, and not adopt another order such as 2, 1, 3. This means that the number of orders of all the classes at a given level is simply the factorial of the number of differences introduced, and not this factorial to the power of the number of arrays, because for each possible order of the first array there is now only one possible order for each of the other arrays. This means that with our simple scheme discussed above, at the first level there are 3! possible orders, at the 2nd level there are also 3! orders, and at the 3rd level 3! orders again, so that the total number of hierarchies, without taking into account the order in chain is $3! \times 3! \times 3! = (3!)^3$. Taking into account the order in chain, this number must be multiplied by 3! again, so the total number is $(3!)^4$. For the general case the total number of hierarchies possible with x characteristics generating x differences each, with order of application of characteristics taken into account, but with order in array being common to all arrays at a particular level, is $(x!)^{x+1}$.

Now this is a much more realistic figure, as we are not likely to use different orders for the arrangement of classes within different arrays when these classes have been formed by the repeated application of the same set of differences. The figure is, nevertheless, of a very high order, and for our particular case of 3 characteristics with 3 differences is $(3!)^{3+1} = 6^4 = 1296$ hierarchies. This case is one of a ridiculously small number of characteristics and differences, and in practical classification schemes the numbers concerned are such that the figure for the number of possible hierarchies is still likely to be astronomical. It should be pointed out that this demonstration of the figures involved is based on a gross over-simplification of the case. The likelihood of having a scheme with a given number of characteristics x, each generating the same number, x, differences is remote indeed. In practice the number of differences derived is likely to differ greatly from one characteristic to another, and the existence of a characteristic or characteristics whose differences equal the total number of characteristics will be coincidental. No purpose would be served in complicating the discussion, for this, the simplest of cases, demonstrates the order of magnitude of the problem.

We have considered here an 'enumerative' scheme for the purpose of calculation. It was pointed out in chapter 2 that the end result of scheduling all the terms in a faceted classification in the combinations permitted by the preferred order is an enumerative classification. The number of possible hierarchies is therefore the same for a faceted scheme as it is for an enumerative scheme. There is however another factor which enters into the question of arrangement of classes relative one to another in a faceted scheme, and this is the facility, also mentioned in chapter 2, for combining only some of the elements which comprise a pre-determined class number in an enumerative scheme. Thus in the classification shown above, we could combine the elements B and C, without being obliged to use 1, 2 or 3. In the filing of entries we should have in the enumerative scheme:

B3a
B3b
B3c
C
C1 etc.

In the faceted scheme we could have:

B3a
B3b
B3c
Bc
C
C1 etc.

Thus with a faceted scheme, whilst we can no longer strictly talk of 'hierarchies', the number of possible arrangements of the classes can be still further increased.

It was stressed in chapter 2 that the value of bibliographical classification, if it has any at all lies in its grouping classes in a useful relationship one to another. If it does no more than formulate classes, then it does not serve its intended purpose. If, as is often the case, different groupings for different purposes are required at different times, then classification, be it 'enumerative' or 'faceted' is unlikely to be superior to a non-classified arrangement. *The fantastically large number of possible arrangements of classes is the principle reason why classification applied in the conventional way, that is by assigning a class number to a piece of information and storing the information at a single point determined by the layout of the particular classification scheme, is inadequate for modern information retrieval systems.* Where so many alternatives are possible, the relative position of subjects in the scheme of things can hardly have significance except in those cases where the order is a universally recognised one and no alternative grouping is likely to be required.

Once we have admitted that classification schemes fail on these grounds, there is no redeeming feature which gives cause for entertaining the possibility of justifying their use.

The idea of the useful display of relations between classes has disappeared and the supposed advantage of classification schemes has therefore gone. Chapter 2 endeavoured to draw the important distinction between mere class-making and class making plus arrangement between the classes. If we have lost the potential advantage of the latter we may as well have a non-classified arrangement such as the alphabetical subject catalogue. Assuming that we have an arrangement wherein the significance of order between classes has been abandoned, we might enquire whether the classes themselves have any inherent virtue, though we are no longer concerned with classification in the bibliographical sense.

It would obviously be useful to have all the entries for a specific subject grouped at a single place, and this is, of course, what all conventional systems set out to achieve. How well does the classification shown in figure 2 of chapter 2 do this? If we require all the information on 2-engined bombers, or on low-wing, single engined fighters, we have it neatly grouped at a single place. If, however, we require everything on high-wing aeroplanes, we must search in no fewer than nine places, because the order in which the characteristics were applied leaves division by the 'wing-position' characteristic until last. Here is a case where on one occasion division by characteristics in one order is required and on another occasion division by characteristics in another order is called for. The number of possibilities in this respect is, of course, quite different from the figures for alternative hierarchies discussed above. The number of classes whose specification includes a given difference is the product of the numbers of differences used at each and all of the levels as far down as, but not including, the level at which the difference first appears.

It should be stressed here, that the worst possible picture has been painted in the foregoing discussion, because it has been assumed that every possible order of application of characteristics and every possible order of classes in array is acceptable. Now this assumption is patently false, for the order of breakdown of some subject fields is a foregone conclusion. The breakdown of 'hydrocarbons' shown on page 38 is one which chemists would naturally expect, the breakdown of geographical areas first by continent, then by country, then by state, county, and so on is also an obvious one, and there are clearly many cases where classification is a useful tool, because the number of alternative ways of arranging classes is small. It is for this reason that general schemes meet with a fair degree of success in application. At the other end of the spectrum we have those cases where things are described by a combination of several attributes which exist side by side, and where there cannot possibly be any grounds for selecting one such attribute for citation before another. Personnel records are a case in point, where some of the features at least are quantitative and the attributes therefore completely mutually exclusive, e.g. heights, weights, etc. Because of the nature of this kind of information, and its consequent ease of handling, there has been a tendency in recent years to call it 'data' as distinct from 'information'. The difference in the middle ranges is, however, often one of degree rather than of principle and particular cases must determine whether they are amenable to treatment by means of classification.

If we abandon the idea of classification, we are immediately back with subject specification. If we have a classification scheme which does not bring about useful relationship between classes we are still back with specification, though we may not admit it. Let us now consider what difficulties arise with subject specification when complex subjects are involved. By subject specification we mean the description of the subject concerned in ordinary language, or in code where this is appropriate, so that this description can be stored either (a) in a file whose order is known and recognisable so that the designation can be cited by the searcher and entries bearing it located by reference to the appropriate point in the file, or (b) in a file in random order with a facility for 'sorting through' or 'sequentially scanning' the file in order to select entries bearing the designation. The 'known order' of (a) need not be a classified one and the 'random order' of (b) can be any order and any one order would be a classified one only by the most extraordinary coincidence.

The problem, then, is one of developing a satisfactory indexing language and so organising the file that it is possible to designate a subject in a single unambiguous way and to determine the exact position in an ordered file of entries with that designation, or to recognise such entries when encountered in sorting through a random sequence. We are not concerned here with the problem of indexing language, but with the mechanics of file organisation. Suppose we have a document on 'the stability of supersonic delta wings with podded engines and blown flaps during landing'. We might break this up into the elements:

WINGS—DELTA—SUPERSONIC—PODS—FLAPS—BLOWING—
LANDING—STABILITY

There are three basic ways in which we might cite a designation for search purposes so that this document will be retrieved:

1   We can cite one of the elements above and search for this single term.
2   We can cite all of the elements, so that the search designation is co-extensive with the indexing designation.
3   We can cite more than one, but not all, of the elements.

If our aim is to cater for 1 we can provide all that is necessary by simply making an entry under each of the terms in the subject designation. This sort of provision is often made and an alphabetical subject catalogue whose headings consist of single terms does just this. The number of entries required is simply the equivalent of the number of terms in the designation, and unless this number is very high a conventional multiple entry system should be acceptable.

If the situation is such that a complex heading of the kind shown above is always sought by citing exactly the same terms as the indexer used, the problem is still easier for this requirement 2 is met by a single entry, with provision of course, for a standard order of terms in the designation. There is but one point in an ordered file to which the indexer assigns the entry, and the searcher cannot help but refer to that precise point. This situation is likely to arise very seldom indeed. The chance of a searcher matching exactly all the elements in a compound subject designation of any complexity is very remote. For this reason an orthodox system using specific headings for complete subjects is an unsatisfactory and uneconomic proposition. (The one striking exception to this is the chemical formula index of the kind provided with 'Chemical Abstracts'. The chemist searching by empirical formula is unlikely to be interested in anything but the particular compound which answers exactly to his specified formula.)

This leads us to condition 3 above, which is exactly the requirement which forms the vast majority of requests for retrieval of documents in a special collection. The conventional system is hopelessly inadequate to cater for this need and the newer systems of classification based on facet analysis are equally impotent. It is the difficulty of finding in a file all those entries which include the terms chosen by the searcher, because there are many varieties of designation which the indexer has used, all of which include the required combination of terms, but which are scattered throughout the file because the indexer has interspersed other terms and therefore determined different filing positions. This difficulty is encountered even when comparatively broad headings, by special library standards, are used and the case of a subheading attached to many different main headings spells the beginning of such troubles.

BRIDGES, ARCH	— Design
,, ,,	— Stresses
BRIDGES, CANTILEVER	— Design
,, ,,	— Maintenance
,, ,,	— Stresses
BRIDGES, SUSPENSION	— Building
,, ,,	— Repair
,, ,,	— Stresses

The enquirer looking for information on stresses in bridges in general has to look in as many places as there are kinds of bridge, because he has cited two terms 'bridge' and 'stresses' but other terms denoting the kinds, i.e. 'arch', 'cantilever' and 'suspension' have been interpolated between his chosen terms.

The solution to this problem is, of course, to make as many entries as are necessary to ensure that whatever terms the searcher uses (providing the indexer has used all of these and perhaps more) he will locate the relevant documents at a single place in the file. This is the crux of the whole matter as far as the argument on conventional versus non-conventional systems is concerned, for whatever facilities are built into a non-conventional system, be they role indicators, interfixes, thesaurus-type relationships, categorisation, or any other type of vocabulary control device, a conventional system could be similarly equipped provided the necessary number of entries could be made to ensure one-place reference. If we could achieve one-place reference for all purposes, the use of non-conventional systems could hardly be justified under any circumstances. To mechanise a system of this kind would amount to mechanising the 'direct access' process of conventional catalogue consultation. (This process is called 'random access' in computer language.) Mechanising the process could be justified only on account of the frequency of use being so high as to be too much for human beings to cope with. This is hardly likely to be the case even in the largest libraries. *The failure of conventional systems is due virtually entirely to the impossibility of providing the necessary number of entries to facilitate retrieval in all cases by one-place reference to a file in known order.*

Let us examine the magnitude of the problem. When discussing the virtue of non-conventional systems, it is invariably said that in order to provide all the necessary entries in a conventional file it is necessary to permute the elements in the compound subject designation, thus producing an entry for every permutation. Permutation consists of arranging a given number of unlike things in every possible order and the number of such orders is the factorial of the number of things. Thus the number of ways in which 3 things can be arranged is factorial 3 (written 3!), which is $3 \times 2 \times 1$ ways. Now in spite of the fact that the view that permutation is necessary for this purpose has been held universally since the problem of indexing compound subject designations was first discussed, it is simply not true.

We are concerned not with various orders of things at all, but with the necessity of being able to select a given number of things from a larger number of things, and it is the number of ways in which such selections can be made which is relevant to our problem. This is a matter of combinations, which deals with just this question of the number of ways in which selections of a stated number of things can be made from a larger number of unlike things. The number of ways in which we can select r things at a time from n unlike things is stated thus:

$$_nC_r = \frac{n!}{r!(n-r)!}$$

Taking the first of the three basic ways of citing a designation for search purposes listed above, it was stated that the number of entries necessary to provide for retrieval by any one term was equal to the number of terms in the indexed designation. This is the same thing as saying that the number of required entries is the number of ways of selecting one thing at a time from several unlike things. Similarly the second way, that of citing all of the elements can be said to require a number of entries equal to the number of ways of selecting n things at a time from n unlike things. This number is, of course 1. Finally to cover all the requirements of the third way, we have to add together all the ways of selecting two terms at a time from the total number of terms in the indexed designation, all the ways of selecting three terms, all the ways of selecting four terms, etc.

There is one important point which must be stressed here, and that is that as we are talking of conventional systems such as the alphabetical subject catalogue and the classified catalogue we have to think in terms of the order in which the elements in a compound heading are to be cited. We have abandoned permutation, which concerns itself with orders and the statements above regarding the numbers of entries necessary under given circumstances are made on the assumption that a standard order of terms is always adhered to when indexing designations are formulated. This order can, of course, be any order as long as it is consistently used and alphabetical order or the notational order of a classification scheme will serve. *We can now state that the number of entries necessary for each document in a conventional visible system to ensure retrieval by reference to a single point in the file of all documents whose subject designations comprise or include all the elements cited by the searcher, provided a standard order of citation of elements in designations is used, is the sum of all the combinations of 1 from n, 2 from n, 3 from n . . . n from n, where n equals the number of elements in a document's subject designation:*

$$n_{C_1} + n_{C_2} + n_{C_3} \ldots + n_{C_n}$$

This can be expressed simply as $2^n - 1$

Let us take a simple example to demonstrate the working of this principle. A suitable subject might be 'the lift produced by blown flaps during take-off'. The elements in the compound heading can be considered to be LIFT, BLOWING, FLAPS, TAKE-OFF. As we have to cite each combination in a standard order, alphabetical order is the obvious one to use and we may as well cite them in this order before we begin to make selections:

BLOWING: FLAPS: LIFT: TAKE-OFF

The total number of entries necessary is $_4C_1 + _4C_2 + _4C_3 + _4C_4 = 4 + 6 + 4 + 1 = 15$. The first group of combinations $_4C_1$ is of course each of the four terms cited above:

BLOWING
FLAPS
LIFT
TAKE-OFF

The second group $_4C_2$ consists of every selection of 2 from 4:

> BLOWING: FLAPS
> BLOWING: LIFT
> BLOWING: TAKE-OFF
> FLAPS: LIFT
> FLAPS: TAKE-OFF
> LIFT: TAKE-OFF

The third group $_4C_3$ consists of every selection of 3 from 4:

> BLOWING: FLAPS: LIFT
> BLOWING: FLAPS: TAKE-OFF
> BLOWING: LIFT: TAKE-OFF
> FLAPS: LIFT: TAKE-OFF

The fourth group $_4C_4$ consists of the single case of every selection of 4 from 4:

> BLOWING: FLAPS: LIFT: TAKE-OFF

Arranging these fifteen entries in alphabetical order as they would be filed in the conventional visible file, we have:

1 BLOWING
2 BLOWING: FLAPS
3 BLOWING: FLAPS: LIFT
4 BLOWING: FLAPS: LIFT: TAKE-OFF
5 BLOWING: FLAPS: TAKE-OFF
6 BLOWING: LIFT
7 BLOWING: LIFT: TAKE-OFF
8 BLOWING: TAKE-OFF
9 FLAPS
10 FLAPS: LIFT
11 FLAPS: LIFT: TAKE-OFF
12 FLAPS: TAKE-OFF
13 LIFT
14 LIFT: TAKE-OFF
15 TAKE-OFF

Here we have all the entries which this method would produce for a document to which four terms or elements were assigned in indexing. Bearing in mind that our purpose is to provide for certain retrieval by reference to a single place in the file regardless of whether we search for any one, two, three or all four of the terms, let us look again at the nature of these entries. Suppose we seek information on 'lift produced by flaps'. The relevant search terms are obviously 'lift' and 'flaps' and if we arrange these in alphabetical order FLAPS : LIFT and consult the file at this point, we find that there are two relevant entries, one comprising the two terms and nothing more, the other comprising the two terms plus the term 'take-off'. The philosophy of these principles has been based on the premise that we will accept any entry provided it includes the search terms, regardless of whether any additional terms appear with them. Indeed, our purpose is to make this specific provision and it is this which conventional systems do not normally give, and which is the very *raison d'être* of non-conventional systems.

As these two entries (Nos. 10 and 11) are for the same document, it is clear that one of them is unnecessary, for either would ensure retrieval in this particular search. It is also clear that at another time we might search for 'lift of flaps at take-off' and if we dispense with entry No. 11 we shall cause non-retrieval of the document for this search. We can, however, dispense with entry No. 10 for entry No. 11 will serve both purposes. We can now introduce a further principle to cut the number of entries required still further, and this is that all designations which form the beginning of larger designations can be dispensed with.

This means that entries Nos. 1, 2, 3, 6, 9, 10 and 13 need not be made, for in every case another entry consists of the terms cited consecutively, i.e. without other terms interpolated, with one or more additional terms following. Thus entry 4 consists of entry 3 plus 'take-off'. It also consists of entry 2 plus 'lift' and 'take-off' and of entry 1 plus 'flaps', 'lift' and 'take-off'. The entries in this list of fifteen which remain after this operation are Nos. 4, 5, 7, 8, 11, 12, 14 and

15. The number of entries required for a document with a subject designation consisting of four terms is therefore eight. In fact the simple rule is that for a document with a designation consisting of n terms the number of entries is $2^{(n-1)}$. *We can therefore qualify our earlier statement and say that the number of entries necessary for each document in a conventional visible system to ensure retrieval by reference to a single point in the file of all documents whose subject designations comprise or include all the elements cited by the searcher, provided a standard order of citation of elements in designations is used, is $2^{(n-1)}$, where n equals the number of elements in a document's subject designation.*

The entries remaining after application of the principle to the list above are:

BLOWING: FLAPS: LIFT: TAKE-OFF

BLOWING: FLAPS: TAKE-OFF

BLOWING: LIFT: TAKE-OFF

BLOWING: TAKE-OFF

FLAPS: LIFT: TAKE-OFF

FLAPS: TAKE-OFF

LIFT: TAKE-OFF

TAKE-OFF

No matter what combination of the used terms is cited by the searcher, these eight entries will ensure retrieval in every case. If we accepted the contention that permutation of the terms is necessary, the number of entries in this case would be twenty-four. Reduction by using all combinations as discussed earlier would reduce this number to fifteen and our final reduction has brought the number down to eight. A designation with a small number of elements has been deliberately used here to enable an actual demonstration to be made, but increased numbers of elements soon increase the numbers of permutations which would be required to astronomical figures. Comparative figures of the number of entries needed by permutation, by providing all combinations and by the use of the system described here are shown overleaf:

No of elements in designation	Permutations $(n!)$	All combinations $2^n - 1$	New system $2^{(n-1)}$
2	2	3	2
3	6	7	4
4	24	15	8
5	120	31	16
6	720	63	32
7	5,040	127	64
8	40,320	255	128
9	362,880	511	256
10	3,628,800	1023	512

Now the purpose of this discussion has been to show the impossibility of catering for complex subjects in conventional systems on account of the prohibitive number of entries required. There is little wonder that conventional systems have been found unacceptable for these purposes, particularly as the number of entries required by permutation has been the criterion by which the situation has been appraised. The argument against conventional systems is not invalidated by the principles introduced here, for the number of entries required in many cases where complex subjects are concerned is still too high to be acceptable. Consideration of these principles does however allow a re-orientation of the problem, for it permits a considerable shift of the point on the scale at which we might consider conventional systems still in the running. If we had, for instance, a system in which we took a maximum of five or six terms assigned to a document for indexing purposes to be adequate, we should undoubtedly reject the idea of using a conventional system if we considered the number of entries which permutation demands, i.e. 120 and 720 respectively. The numbers demanded for five or six term designations by the method advocated here would be sixteen and thirty-two respectively. These are somewhat high for conventional systems produced by conventional methods, but the idea of a 'printed combination index' which would be of conventional visible alphabetical index form, but which might be produced by using a computer, is not so unrealistic.

An experiment is in fact being conducted in the writer's own organisation with designations of a maximum of five terms, using punched cards and an IBM 1401 computer. A detailed description of this index is given in the appendix at the end of this book.

It might be useful here to describe a very simple method of determining how the $2^{(n-1)}$ designations are made up from the terms assigned to a document in indexing, for there may be cases where the principle might usefully be applied in a manually-compiled system, and it is also useful for programming a punched card operation or a computer. We achieved this objective in the description given above by actually deriving and listing all the relevant combinations and deleting the unwanted ones. The final list can be achieved directly by first listing the terms assigned to a document in the standard order (we will use alphabetical order) and applying the following pair of rules repeatedly until all the terms have been used.

1   Add the next term to all existing designations.
2   Repeat all the designations so formed, deleting the penultimate term in each case.

The following is an example of the procedure applied to five terms A, B, C, D, E. Taking the first term A, we apply the first rule which means adding A to nothing, which means setting it down alone:

> A

We cannot apply the second rule here because there is no penultimate term. Taking the first rule again we add B to A:

> AB

Applying rule 2 we repeat this designation, removing A, which gives us B. Total designations are now:

> AB
> B

Applying rule 1 we convert these to

> ABC
> BC

Applying rule 2 gives us AC and C. Total designations are now

        ABC
        BC
        AC
        C

Rule 1 gives us ABCD, BCD, ACD and CD. Rule 2 gives us ABD, BD, AD, D. Total designations are now

        ABCD
        BCD
        ACD
        CD
        ABD
        BD
        AD
        D

Finally rule 1 gives us ABCDE, BCDE, ACDE, CDE, ABDE, BDE ADE and DE. Rule 2 gives us ABCE, BCE, ACE, CE, ABE, BE, AE and E. Total designations, arranged in alphabetical order are

        ABCDE
        ABCE
        ABDE
        ABE
        ACDE
        ACE
        ADE
        AE
        BCDE
        BCE
        BDE
        BE
        CDE
        CE
        DE
        E

There are certain difficulties which arise in the practical use of a visible index so compiled and these are described in the account of the computer-based system given in the appendix.

The whole of the foregoing discussion on providing for matching subject designations for retrieval purposes has centred on the problem of 'what you put in and what you leave out', for if the searcher always put in what the indexer put in and no more, we should be concerned with $_nC_n$ entries for a document in all cases, i.e. a single entry, and conventional systems would always meet the case. We have to face this problem, however for this ideal state of affairs rarely exists, and the difficulty appears whenever 'multi-topical' subjects arise, including their appearance in classification schemes. The problem is seen perhaps as clearly as anywhere in the 'chain index' to a faceted classification scheme. It was mentioned in chapter 2 that the facility provided by a faceted classification scheme of enabling terms to be selected from only some of the relevant facets as distinct from the obligation of fitting a subject into a ready-made number in an enumerative scheme is a snare and a delusion. This is again explained by the principle of 'what you put in and what you leave out'.

The subject mentioned earlier in this chapter 'the stability of supersonic delta wings with podded engines and blown flaps during landing', if it were classified by the faceted classification used for the ASLIB Cranfield Research Project, would take the following notation:

Cd (Ij) Cr Ei Kg Nbk Ob Okd

Chain index entries would then be made as follows:

1   BLOWING: STABILITY: SUPERSONIC FLOW:
    LANDING: PODS: FLAPS: DELTA: WINGS
                        Cd (Ij) Cr Ei Kg Nbk Ob Okd

2   STABILITY: SUPERSONIC FLOW: LANDING: PODS:
    FLAPS: DELTA: WINGS
                        Cd (Ij) Cr Ei Kg Nbk Ob

3 SUPERSONIC FLOW: LANDING: PODS: FLAPS:
DELTA: WINGS   Cd (Ij) Cr Ei Kg Nbk

4 LANDING: PODS: FLAPS: DELTA: WINGS
    Cd (Ij) Cr Ei Kg

5 PODS: FLAPS: DELTA: WINGS
    Cd (Ij) Cr Ei

6 FLAPS: DELTA: WINGS
    Cd (Ij) Cr

7 DELTA: WINGS   Cd (Ij)

8 WINGS   Cd

Clearly provision is made here for searching for an individual element in all the contexts in which it might be found, so that for instance, along with the entry beginning PODS there will be other entries for other documents dealing with pods, each with a series of different terms according to the several different specific subjects of those documents. There are two ways in which combinations of terms can be found in faceted classified catalogues:

(a) The searcher can enter the chain index at the word he chooses for entry word, e.g. PODS, and he can then search through, i.e. sequentially scan, all the entries there to see whether any include the other term or terms he is seeking. He will not find such a term if it happens to appear later in the schedules, e.g. if he looks for STABILITY in the entries under PODS, he cannot possibly find any because if the term has been associated with PODS at all, it will have been deleted by 'chain procedure' by the time entries for PODS are made. This is shown in the entries above, where STABILITY appears in entries 1 and 2 only.

(b) If he finds no entries including both PODS and STABILITY in the chain index he can consult all the points in the classified file to which reference is made from the entries under PODS. If, as is the case here, STABILITY follows PODS in the schedules, he may find entries there which include both (and would in fact find the one cited here).

The most satisfactory way would, of course, be to make the process of consultation a more positive one by turning up the two terms in the schedules to determine the order in which they appear and then taking one or other of these two courses, using whichever term is appropriate to the course chosen. The whole point is that whether we are searching in the chain index or in the classified file we are sequentially scanning under a single term and only a non-conventional system, or provision of the necessary number of additional entries in a visible file can overcome this difficulty.

It may well be that in the construction of an alphabetical index for a classified catalogue based on a faceted classification scheme we have the ideal application for the printed combinated index, provided that the length of class numbers for documents never exceeds, say, five elements. We shall examine here the kind of index so produced and for this purpose we shall assume that we are going to arrange the terms forming each entry in alphabetical order, which is the simplest way, but it would be possible to preserve the 'reverse of schedule' order of the chain index type of entry provided we were prepared to check the schedules to determine the order of terms before we carried out a search. The example which we shall consider will be based on the ASLIB Cranfield Research Project faceted classification scheme.

Suppose we have the subject 'the buckling of rectangular aluminium plates in compression'. The class symbol for this subject is Ffe (Ikb) Peal Rkh Rqg and the terms from the schedules, arranged in alphabetical order are:

Aluminium: Buckling: Compression: Plates: Rectangular

Entries are made according to the rules for a printed combination index, and each entry refers to the full class symbol, not merely to the elements for which terms appear in the entry as is the case with the chain index. The full set of entries for this subject is:

1	Aluminium:	Buckling:	Compression:	Plates:	Rectangular
2	Aluminium:	Buckling:	Compression:	Rectangular
3	Aluminium:	Buckling:	Plates:	Rectangular
4	Aluminium:	Buckling:	Rectangular
5	Aluminium:	Compression:	Plates:	Rectangular
6	Aluminium:	Compression:	Rectangular
7	Aluminium:	Plates:	Rectangular
8	Aluminium:	Rectangular
9	Buckling:	Compression:	Plates:	Rectangular
10	Buckling:	Compression:	Rectangular
11	Buckling:	Plates:	Rectangular
12	Buckling:	Rectangular
13	Compression:	Plates:	Rectangular
14	Compression:	Rectangular
15	Plates:	Rectangular
16	Rectangular

The resulting index would then have entries each of which might list any number of different class symbols in which the sought terms were included. For example entry No. 7 above might appear thus:

```
Aluminium:  Plates:  Rectangular

   Bef Ea Ffe (Ikb) Peal
   Byd Ffe (Ikb) Peal
   Cd Ffe (Ikb) Peal Qm
   Ffe (Ikb) Fkm Peal Rm
   Ffe (Ikb) Peal Rkh Rqg
   Ffe (Ikb) Peal Rkm
```

The subjects of the class symbols referred to here are respectively:

Rectangular aluminium plates in the hulls of flying boats

Rectangular aluminium plates in rigid airships

Rivetting rectangular aluminium plates in wings

Stresses in rectangular aluminium plates in monocoque structures

Buckling of rectangular aluminium plates in compression

Fatigue in rectangular aluminium plates

The enquirer seeking information on 'rectangular aluminium plates' would thus be referred to these several points in the classified file where he would find entries for documents on these several subjects, any or all of which might be relevant. Producing so many entries by hand would be a laborious procedure, but as the size of the index grew much of the work would consist of the addition of new class numbers to existing entries. The obvious solution would be to mechanise the whole procedure.

It hardly needs to be pointed out that as an alternative to this scheme it would be possible to use the principle of the printed combination index to provide multiple entries in the classified file instead of in the alphabetical index. The class numbers would be processed for this purpose and the alphabetical index need consist of no more than a schedule of individual terms, each with its notational element.

Faceted classification with chain indexing has been advocated as a solution to the problem of dealing with complex subjects, and it is undoubtedly easier to assign a synthetic notation than it is to place a complex subject in an enumerative classification scheme, but the point is that finding the complex subject for retrieval is not one wit easier. It is very difficult to understand why such store has been set by these methods, and there is now some realisation of their shortcomings. Farradane said fairly recently, 'As long as a chain index is considered an integral part of facet methods, such

systems may be at a disadvantage'.[2] Jean Aitchison has also
shown a practical example of these difficulties by listing some
of the entries under 'Fatigue' in the chain index to the classified catalogue of the Group Central Library of the English
Electric Co.[3] There has been a great deal of loose talk, particularly since the results of the tests on the first stage of the
Cranfield Research Project were made known, about the cause
of the poor showing of the faceted classification used being
due to rigid adherence to a preferred order, with the suggestion
that a more flexible approach, with facility for permutation
as desired would have meant a better result. There are
undoubtedly cases where such facility would have made for
more satisfactory synthesis of class symbols, but the foregoing discussion has shown that the most economic provision
of multiple entry for a conventional visible file, with assurance
of certain matching with one-place reference is based on taking advantage of preferred order and we should not blame it
for something of which it is not guilty. It is not the fault of
preferred order, but the problem of combinations of terms from
a larger number of terms. It should not be forgotten, of course,
that the purpose of the 'preferred order' in a faceted scheme
is to display to the best advantage the relations between the
terms. The remoteness of the possibility of finding such an
order which will meet all purposes was demonstrated
theoretically earlier in this chapter, and experience has shown
that this is indeed a practical problem. It is also true that
some flexibility, rather than a rigid order, can produce more
satisfactory class symbols for the various cases which are likely
to be met. All this is, however, academic if we cannot find the
relevant terms in association at all. When we have catered
for this problem we can begin to think of the more
sophisticated problems of showing subject relationships, and
physical juxtaposition of elements by flexibility of order is
not the only way of achieving this. If, however, the classificationists insist on preferred order in faceted classification
schemes, then it is worth noting that with the system
advanced here we have the best of both worlds, for we
preserve the preferred order then actually exploit it to provide

a minimum number of entries, extravagant as this number might seem when compared with the number used in the inefficient chain index.

Another indication of the realisation of the inadequacy of the chain index is the suggestion put forward by Foskett[4] that there should be no progressive removal of terms in formulating the series of entries which are to appear in the chain index, but that all terms should appear in all entries, with one card filed under each of the individual terms. In fact Foskett has adopted this principle but has transferred these 'multiple entries' to the classified file where an entry appears at the appropriate place under each of the elements concerned. This is some improvement, of course, in that at one place in the classified file there will appear all the entries which include the chosen element. But the point is that we are still trying to find combinations of terms by starting with one of the terms only and we are still up against sequential scanning of that block of entries. This method is still, therefore, no substitute for the more efficient non-conventional systems.

Another method which has appeared recently is the KWIC (keyword in context) index. This system is usually based on the titles of documents and is produced by feeding titles in machine-readable form into a computer which will produce a heading for each 'keyword' in the title, arrange these headings in alphabetical order by keywords and print out the resulting series with the keywords down the centre of the column. The heading does in fact consist of the title, or more usually a part of the title because of the limited space available, positioned so that the keyword is so placed, and depending on this positioning and the length of the title the tail end may be brought round to the front of the entry, or the beginning may appear at the end. This is of course a 'cycling' process and KWIC provides in plain language a searching facility similar to that of Foskett's 'rotated' index, though the latter shifts the notation laterally on the line without any 'wrap around'. KWIC indexing is typified by the American Chemical Society's bi-weekly *Chemical Titles*, a typical group of entries from which appears as follows:

as studied by electron SPIN resonance.= spatial distribution
tassium ferri cyanide.= SPIN-lattice relaxation time measur
in canted spin arrays.= SPIN-wave contribution to specific h
ion of the heart of the SPINAL dog by phen oxy benz amine.=
ncing factor from human SPINAL fluid.* an assay method for c
  pigment bodies of the SPINAL neurones of some teleosts.=
a— catalyst.= effect of SPINAL formation on the regenerabili
f furfural in distilled SPIRITS.= determination o
of hexoses in distilled SPIRITS.= estimation
on of oxygen on freshly SPLIT graphite surface.= chemical an

Here we have another case of the unfortunate use of
terminology, for KWIC indexes are being referred to, e.g. by
Kent,[5] as 'permutation indexes'. In one sense in which the
dictionary defines 'permutation' we might regard the word
as acceptable for this purpose, but it does seem extraordinary
that we should use a term in this way when it has already
been established for a long time in the field of information
retrieval as meaning what it means in mathematics, that is
the problem of the alternative orders in which unlike things
can be arranged. If there is one thing which we have not got
here it is alternative orders, for the title in each KWIC entry
is preserved in its original order. Again we have a perfectly
suitable term for the process involved here and that is
'cycling'. The 'cyclic latin square' shows perfectly what takes
place in formulating entries for this type of index:

A	B	C	D	E
B	C	D	E	A
C	D	E	A	B
D	E	A	B	C
E	A	B	C	D

If the letters A, B, C, D, E, are regarded as the terms in the
designation, each horizontal line shows the form of one

entry. The first column of the square might be regarded as containing the entry word in each case.

KWIC indexing suffers from the fatal weakness of conventional systems in that sequential scanning under the selected entry word is necessary, and it is non-conventional only in the way in which it is produced. As a tool for the user it is certainly not novel. Exactly the same facility was provided by the catalogue produced for the Manchester Free Library by Crestadoro in 1864. The Manchester catalogue differed only in that it was produced manually and not by a computer, and in that the actual form of the heading was not precisely the same. It served just as well to locate entries by citing a single 'keyword' from the title. KWIC indexing does, of course, serve a useful purpose on the principle that half a loaf is better than no bread, and it is better to have *Chemical Titles* than nothing at all between the publication of an article and its appearance in *Chemical Abstracts*. It is the poorest possible form of indexing from the user's point of view and its limitations should be recognised. The idea of using a five-year cumulation of *Chemical Titles* will hardly bear thinking about.

All this is bound up with the basic retrieval problem of being able to select simultaneously several elements in a compound subject designation. Provision for retrieval by citing only one term at a time, no matter how economically it might be done by mechanisation does not meet the user's needs and systems based on this principle are therefore unacceptable for modern retrieval requirements. This is the reason why conventional systems are inadequate for many current needs. This chapter has shown how an appraisal of the necessity or otherwise of a non-conventional system can be made in those cases in the middle ranges where the number of added entries necessary to make the conventional system efficient may not be prohibitive.

There is one other factor which we must consider in this respect. Assuming that we have the prospect of sequential scanning in a conventional system, we must consider how much such scanning must be done in the average search. This depends on the ratio of the number of terms in the vocabulary to the number of documents in the collection. Suppose we have a collection of 100,000 documents and a vocabulary of 100 terms and that all terms are used equally often. Suppose also that the number of terms assigned to each document is 5. The total number of terms actually used in the system will be 500,000, and as we have only 100 separate terms, this means that any one term is assigned to 5,000 documents. If we make an entry for a document under each of its 5 terms there will be 5,000 separate entries under any one term. Clearly this would be unacceptable under any circumstances, for we could not consider sorting through 5,000 entries each time we made a search. A non-conventional system is obviously essential.

If we have the same size of collection, i.e. 100,000 documents with the same number of terms used for each document, i.e. 5, but with a vocabulary of 10,000 terms instead of 100, the result is very much different. The number of separate entries under any one term now becomes 50 and this might not be an unacceptably high number of entries to sort through for a search for ordinary retrieval purposes. A non-conventional system might not be considered essential here.

In considering the statistical aspect of the choice of a retrieval system a start should be made by assessing (a) the potential size of the collection (b) the potential size of the vocabulary and (c) the average number of terms to be assigned to a document. On the assumption that an entry is to be made under each of the terms assigned to a document it is then possible to calculate how many entries under a given entry word would need to be sorted through to exhaust every possibility of finding a given combination of terms. If the number is acceptable, a conventional visible file should be adequate. If the number of entries is too high for a conventional system to be acceptable, the possibility of increasing the number of entries per document to $2^{(n-1)}$ should be considered, for this will reduce retrieval time by eliminating sorting through and thus giving one-place reference. If the cost of producing a system on this basis is too high, then a non-conventional system should be considered.

It is clear from the foregoing that a decision between adoption of a conventional or a non-conventional system need not be guesswork. There are other factors which enter into the question and different circumstances demand different treatments, but it would seem that the philosophy outlined above is seldom taken into account in designing retrieval systems. It is difficult to understand, for instance, why an edge-punched card system should have been adopted in the case described by Cawkell.[6] This article is a most useful and interesting account of the problems of coding for punched card purposes, but the curious feature is that the subject designations to be coded were to be limited to four and perhaps even three elements! With the method described here designations of three elements would be catered for by four cards in an alphabetical subject catalogue instead of the three punched cards in the system described. Admittedly provision is made for retrieval by authors, date, and various kinds of form, but it seems unlikely that a system of this kind can be justified for these particular requirements.

The argument of this chapter has been firstly that classification schemes, be they 'enumerative' or 'faceted' cannot cater for all modern retrieval requirements because various 'hierarchies' are required for various purposes and the number of possible hierarchies is so high as to preclude the possibility of determining one order which will meet all requirements. The flexibility of faceted systems is of little or no advantage because though designations can be 'tailor-made' for documents the problem of finding the designation is not eased. This is not to be construed as meaning that facet analysis has no value; on the contrary the best possible system may consist of a vocabulary based on facet analysis and used as a 'co-ordinate' system. Secondly, when we concern ourselves with subject specification conventional systems fail because of the difficulty of searching for combinations of terms which do not coincide in nature and number with the designation assigned by the indexer. The next chapter will deal with the 'non-conventional' methods which overcome this difficulty.

D

REFERENCES

1   Shera, J. H., Classification: current functions and applications to the subject analysis of library materials. In *The subject analysis of library materials*, edited by M. F. Tauber, School of Library Service, Columbia University, New York, 1953, p. 31.

2   Farradane, J. The challenge of information retrieval. *Journal of Documentation*, Vol. 17, No. 4, December 1961, pp. 233-44.

3   Aitchison, Jean. English Electric Company. Part IV of Classification Research Group Bulletin, No. 7. In *Journal of Documentation*, Vol. 18, No. 2, June 1962, pp. 65-88.

4   Foskett, D. J. Two notes on indexing techniques. I: Rotated indexes. *Journal of Documentation*, Vol. 18, No. 4, December 1962, pp. 188-9.

5   Kent, A. *Textbook on mechanized information retrieval*, Interscience, New York, 1962, p. 117.

6   Cawkell, A. E. Classification and retrieval of technical information. *Wireless World*, Vol. 68, No. 8, August 1962, pp. 352-7; No. 9, September 1962, pp. 432-4.

5

The Advantages of
Non-conventional Systems

The difficulties which beset bibliographical classification cannot be alleviated by the application of non-conventional principles. If circumstances are such that different hierarchies are required to provide different groupings according to the variety of the demands made on the system, a bibliographical classification scheme, be it enumerative or faceted, will be useful in inverse proportion to the number of hierarchies which are potentially useful for the purpose which the system is intended to serve. For many current and future requirements bibliographical classification schemes are patently inadequate and a non-conventional approach, with or without mechanisation, cannot help.

If, however, we consider what might be done with regard to applying non-conventional methods to systems in which we are concerned with subject specification and not with subject classification, the situation is very much different, for what is virtually impossible with conventional systems becomes not only possible but an eminently practicable proposition, often with the simplest equipment. The solution of the problem lies in the application of methods which overcome the difficulties of searching for 'combinations', the theory of which was dealt with at length in the last chapter. These methods are all based on the principle of 'concept co-ordination', an expression whose meaning is currently far too nebulous and which requires to be clearly understood before we can discuss the use of non-conventional systems.

The word 'co-ordination' when used in the expressions 'concept co-ordination' or 'co-ordinate indexing' does not imply co-ordination in the sense in which it is used in mathematics.

We are concerned in information retrieval with co-ordination in the sense in which the word is used in connection with the calculus of classes, and it is useful to introduce some of the most elementary principles of Boolean algebra, which, with the aid of Venn diagrams, illustrates clearly the nature of what we require from a retrieval system.

There are basically three kinds of question which we might ask of a system. The first of these questions consists of a

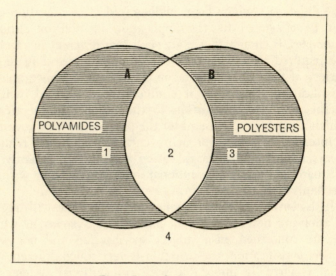

Fig 4 Logical sum A ∪ B

demand for information on one or other of two or more subjects. Thus we might say that we require information on either POLYAMIDES or POLYESTERS, and the Venn diagram shown in figure 4 illustrates this type of request, which is known as a 'logical sum'.

Here the two circles A and B represent respectively the classes of things which are polyamides and polyesters. The whole of the area included in the two circles, that is areas 1, 2 and 3 taken together represent things which are either polyamides or polyesters, or both. Boole himself regarded the logical sum as excluding area 2, but this area, which is common to both A and B, is now considered to be more usefully regarded as included in the logical sum for purposes of symbolic logic. For our purposes, however, it is best to regard the area as excluded, because it has a special significance in our field, which will be dealt with shortly. The shaded area in figure 4 is therefore the relevant one for our definition of a logical sum.

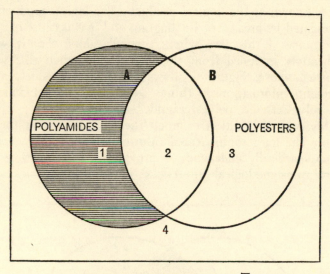

Fig 5 Logical difference A $\cap$ $\overline{B}$

The second kind of question which we might encounter is that which demands information on one of the classes, but specifically states that it must not be information on the other. Thus we might specify that we require information on polyamides, but *not* on polyesters. This is represented by figure 5 and is known as a 'logical difference'. The shaded area again represents the definition of the subject for search. The logical difference represented here is not really typical of search questions, but this form has been used in order to preserve consistency in the diagrams for the sake of simplicity.

A more truly typical question would be that which demanded information on polyamides but not on nylon 6. Nylon 6 is one kind of polyamide and diagrammatically would be represented by a circle within circle A. Nothing is lost, however, in using the diagram as in figure 5, and it is felt that the principle is more easily assimilated if looked at in this way.

The third type of question is that which demands of the system information on things which are both A and B, and this is known as the 'logical product'. The logical product is represented by area 2 in the diagram and it is because of the importance of this area when it stands alone that it was deliberately excluded from the logical sum when this was discussed above. Figure 6 shows the logical product, and represents information on things which are both polyamides and polyesters, i.e. polyesteramides.

This type of question is much the most important for it is only the most sophisticated information retrieval systems which specifically endeavour to provide for interrogation by logical sums and logical differences, though it is possible, even

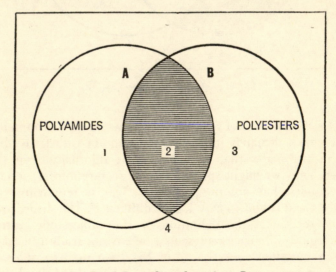

Fig 6 Logical product A ∩ B

with the simplest systems, to conduct searches on these bases if so desired. Our most pressing need, is however for a system which will enable us to search for things which possess any number of attributes, by specifying those attributes at searching. These 'attributes' can, of course, be any features which contribute to defining the subject of search and the logical product of the terms comprising the subject used as an example in chapter 4 is the definition of the required subject:

WINGS—DELTA—SUPERSONIC—PODS—FLAPS—BLOWING—
LANDING—STABILITY

If we ignore the problems of provision for searching for logical sums and logical differences and can solve the problem of providing for retrieval by the logical product of any number of the elements of a subject designation which are used in indexing, then we have solved the major problem. This is in fact, the problem discussed in the last chapter, i.e. the problem of 'combinations', but because non-conventional systems have been seen potentially to be capable of providing for searching on the basis of logical sums, differences and products, the expression 'co-ordinate indexing' is now well established. *The reason why non-conventional systems are to be preferred to conventional systems for some applications is simply that they are capable of providing for selection by some and not necessarily all, of the terms used in indexing. Though this is a matter of combinations, and such indexing might perhaps be better called 'combination indexing', the principle of 'logical products' of the selected terms is a legitimate way of regarding the method and as logical sums and logical differences can also be provided for, the expression 'co-ordinate indexing' is now generally used for systems which make such provision.*

Before passing on to consider the kinds of systems and equipment which can be used to apply co-ordinate principles, it might be of interest to digress for a moment here in order to observe how Venn diagrams illustrate the philosophy of the number of entries required in a visual system in order to provide the same facility as is provided in non-conventional systems. The argument put forward in the last chapter was that the number of entries required in a visual system was not that demanded by permutation, but a considerably smaller number determined by taking every combination of every number of terms from the total terms used in indexing, i.e.

$$_nC_1 + _nC_2 + _nC_3 \ldots + _nC_n = 2^n - 1$$

and then reducing this number still further by eliminating those entries which formed the beginning of larger entries so that the final and minimum number of entries is $2^{(n-1)}$,

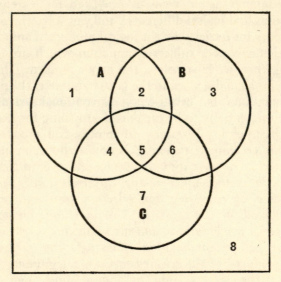

Fig 7 Venn diagram to illustrate combinations
and selected combinations

provided that we use a standard order of citation of terms in headings.

For the purpose of illustrating this diagrammatically we will take a Venn diagram of three classes. This is shown in figure 7.

It will be seen that here we have a total of 8 separate areas within the square and, in fact, the number of sub-classes (our 'areas' in the diagram) is always 2^n, where n is the number of classes.[1] The square represents the 'universe of discourse' in symbolic logic and is an essential part of diagrammatic representation in this context. The only parts which are designated for our purpose, however, are those areas contained within the circles and the non-included part represented by the figure 8 is irrelevant because it signifies only the negation of what is included in the circles. Negation is important in symbolic logic, but the negation of the total of our designated classes is meaningless in terms of subject designations for retrieval search purposes. Thus we are concerned with the areas numbered 1 to 7 and these are in fact representative of the combinations $_3C_1 + _3C_2 + _3C_3$, which is equal to $2^3 - 1$, the '$- 1$' representing the area outside the designated classes, or in this case our area 8. The 7 combinations (which can be extracted from the diagram) are:

$$\text{Area } 1 = A$$
$$,, \quad 2 = AB$$
$$,, \quad 3 = B$$
$$,, \quad 4 = AC$$
$$,, \quad 5 = ABC$$
$$,, \quad 6 = BC$$
$$,, \quad 7 = C$$

Still more interesting is the fact that all those areas which fall completely within the last named class (that is the circle representing class C of our three classes, A, B, C) represent the designations required to give us the absolute minimum of $2^{(n-1)}$ entries for certain retrieval by one-place reference in a visual system:

$$ABC = \text{Area } 5$$
$$AC = \quad ,, \quad 4$$
$$BC = \quad ,, \quad 6$$
$$C = \quad ,, \quad 7$$

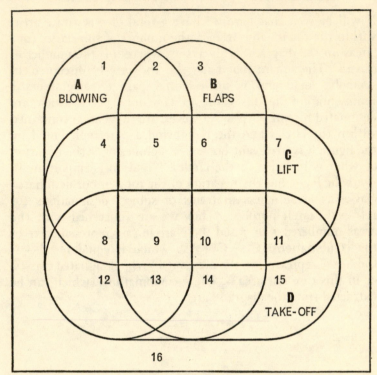

Fig 8 Venn diagram showing four named classes

Figure 8 shows a case of four classes, which is the maximum which can be shown with a simple diagram and even here the circles have had to be stretched to oblong shape. The classes have been designated LIFT, BLOWING, FLAPS and TAKE-OFF.

If we take all the sub-classes which are included in the oblong representing the last-named class, i.e. class D, TAKE-OFF, we find that these are exactly those listed on page 83:

BLOWING:	FLAPS:	LIFT:	TAKE-OFF	=	Area	9
BLOWING:	FLAPS:	TAKE-OFF		=	,,	13
BLOWING:	LIFT:	TAKE-OFF		=	,,	8
BLOWING:	TAKE-OFF			=	,,	12

FLAPS: LIFT: TAKE-OFF	=	Area 10
FLAPS: TAKE-OFF	=	,, 14
LIFT: TAKE-OFF	=	,, 11
TAKE-OFF	=	,, 15

We can now turn from theory and consider the nature of non-conventional systems and the equipment used for their application. It can be said at once that the reason that these newer systems are successful where conventional methods fail is that they solve the problem of 'combinations' by employing methods which make the compilation and maintenance of the necessary records a manageable process whereas the extension of multiple entry in conventional systems would be so costly in labour, and the resulting store so bulky and unwieldy as to make the proposition quite impracticable.

Other considerations are often put forward as reasons for adopting non-conventional systems, but there is little evidence to justify the philosophy behind some of these claims. One argument is that space is paramount and that the size of the store in the system is therefore critical. There is little doubt that if the largest orthodox library catalogues were found to be doing their jobs properly, their replacement would not be considered on the grounds of space-saving. Even the size of actual stocks in libraries is not causing widespread adoption of microreproduction and the outstanding example of a specific decision against microreproduction is that of the National Lending Library for Science and Technology in Great Britain. Whilst space is not at a premium here, the possibilities which storage in microform must have offered in terms of space-saving and manageability must have been staggering. There are, of course, cases where space is absolutely paramount but these are the exception rather than the rule and there can hardly be a legitimate case for non-conventional methods on these grounds. Nevertheless a great deal of the 'hardware' currently being developed in the United States is being directed at this very facet of the problem, apparently with relegation of the really significant problems of subject designation to a subsidiary role.

Another argument often heard is that the infallibility of the electronic computer is the cure for all our ills. It is said that if a computer is set to work to analyse, to store and to retrieve we shall have a situation vastly superior to that in which systems are created by erring humans and that consistency is all that matters. That this consistency can be exploited cannot be denied, and some of the work which is reported in chapter 8 has shown that the matching of a question with full texts can be done better by a machine than it can be done by a human being, on this very basis. This process is carried out, however, on a purely statistical principle. If statistical methods, which can detect similarity of meaning in two texts without being concerned with what that meaning is, prove to be inadequate, then the problem is formidable indeed for it seems that resort will have to be made to a much more complex kind of analysis.

Computers have until the present time been used almost entirely on an algorithmic basis, that is they have been provided with instructions to carry out a series of logical steps in a specified order, without there being any possibility of ambiguity or of a course of action being taken which was not specified by the programmer. Thus the user of a computer can forecast exactly what will happen at any point in the programme. It is clearly necessary to have a clear understanding of what steps must be carried out in order to solve a problem or to attain a specified objective, for only on this basis can an algorithm be devised on which the machine can operate. It is also clear that we have no such understanding of the processes of human thought and it is therefore impossible at the present time to process language by the use of algorithms. We can do all sorts of things with computers but there is no point in using them to do to perfection a job which is useless to us. As McCormick said 'A computer is *objective* in its operations. It will be repeatable in what it does. If given a certain amount of information about a document, it will always index that document in the same way. Thus it will index a document in a *precise* manner although how accurately is another consideration.'[2]

There is however, hope that there may be methods of operating computers other than those which are algorithmic. These are known as 'heuristic' techniques and they differ from algorithmic methods in that the computer is not given a detailed unambiguous course to follow, but is given a certain amount of instruction and is thereafter left to find out for itself what course it ought to take to achieve known objectives. The word 'heuristic' does in fact mean 'serving to find out'. It is still difficult to see how such techniques might be applied to so complex a problem as ours, but enquiry into these methods is very much in its infancy and it is impossible to foresee what benefits may accrue from their development. The paper by McCormick referred to above is an extremely interesting summary of computer potentialities.

A third reason given for the use of non-conventional systems is that they facilitate the mechanisation of information retrieval, with the implication that mechanisation is a good thing for its own sake. Indeed, Jahoda concluded that one of two main advantages claimed for 'correlative' indexing systems was that they lent themselves to mechanisation.[3] Mechanisation should, of course, be applied wherever it makes for the more economical achievement of a given objective, but as was stated in the last chapter, there can hardly be justification for mechanising orthodox catalogue consultation, especially as the laborious part of the operation of such catalogues is their compilation, the very part which we are not yet capable of assigning to machines.

In the present state of the art we should confine ourselves to taking advantage of those features of non-conventional systems which have been shown to be of value. We can base such systems on one of two main principles: item entry or term entry. Item entry systems use a discrete record for each item, which for the time being we can regard as being each document, so that this record bears all the information relating to the document, including its identity and all the 'features' which go to make up its subject designation. Term entry is the inverse of this in that each discrete record is for a feature, or term, and this record bears the identities of all those documents to which the feature has been assigned.

With item entry systems it is necessary to examine each and every entry in the file when a search is made, in order to select those items which match the subject designated for search. There are two ways in which this is normally done, though the difference between the two has little practical significance.

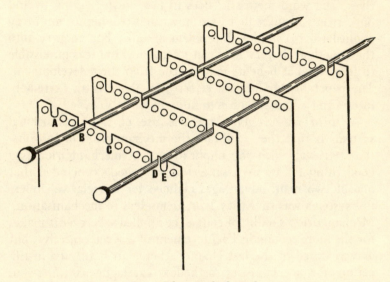

Fig 9 Edge-notched cards

The first is the simultaneous searching of the whole or part of the file, and the only practical manifestation of this is the hand-sorted punched card. Here one or more needles is inserted in the pack and when the pack is lifted with the needle or needles the cards with codings which match the search requirement either drop off completely or to an extent which enables them to be removed from the pack. Figure 9 shows the principle of edge notched cards and it is easy to see from this how punched cards satisfy the requirement of facilitating selection of any combination from the total number of features assigned by the indexer. The first card has five

notches, marked A, B, C, D and E and it is clear that needling
B and D will cause this card to drop.

The other method of searching is not simultaneous but is
'sequential scanning' or 'sorting through'—that is the examination of each record individually in turn, with acceptance or
rejection according to whether the entry matches the search
requirement or not. All item entry systems other than needle-
sorted cards use this principle and perhaps the best known
application is machine-sorted cards, where a library of cards
is passed in its entirety through a sorter which is set to pull
out those cards bearing a particular combination of subject
concepts. The one big disadvantage of item entry is that the
whole file must be searched each time a search is made. This
can be a serious problem on account of the time taken, even
with very fast equipment. With hand sorted punched cards
searching can be very laborious even when the file has grown
to but a few thousand, and with machine sorted cards the
fastest equipment can take hours to process a large file. It is
possible, of course, to break the file up into sections by subject,
date, or some other suitable criterion, but this is not always
desirable and division by subject at once involves us in classification. There is also the problem of card wear with machine-
sorted cards for trouble arises when deterioration of the cards
is sufficient to cause machine stoppages.

Term entry systems are typified by the well-known
'Uniterm' system and optical stencil cards, marketed com-
mercially in the United States as 'Peek-a-boo' cards. 'Uniterm'
systems comprise plain (i.e. not punched) cards, with one
card used for each term in the indexing language. Each such
'feature card' has listed on it the numbers which identify
documents which are relevant to the feature, and for ease
of use the numbers are listed in 'terminal digit' order. This
means that ten columns are provided on the card, the
columns being numbered 0–9, and those document numbers
ending in 0 are posted to the 0 column, those ending in 1 to
the 1 column and so on. Searching consists of withdrawing
from the file the cards for the features which the searcher
has decided are relevant to his requirements and searching for

document numbers which are common to all the cards. Such common numbers represent relevant documents. Figure 10 shows typical Uniterm cards.

Optical stencil cards work in precisely the same way except that numbers common to stacked cards are identified much

WINGS

0	1	2	3	4	5	6	7	8	9
010	201	012	393	304	155	306	527	198	019
320	371	072	643	634	375	616	577	698	299
730	561	272	893	(704)	415	836	1057	738	729
1020	671	782	903	974	615	1866	1087	(668)	999
								08	1049
								28	2069

SPARS

0	1	2	3	4	5	6	7	8	9
080	311	042	053	114	285	136	017	048	099
450	551	292	173	(704)	615	386	467	908	509
690	751	852	553	1024	765	716	537	1498	629
730	991	2012	1063	1114	835	1266	727	(668)	789
								48	1049
								68	2199

FRETTING

0	1	2	3	4	5	6	7	8	9
190	331	012	103	094	185	256	067	048	079
300	571	433	473	(704)	415	496	537	608	509
610	1031	1062	593	744	615	716	1027	1048	769
730		2012		954	1375	1866	1337	(668)	1909
								748	2049
								188	2119

CORROSION

0	1	2	3	4	5	6	7	8	9
080	111	112	093	024	105	056	097	028	149
170	451	782	193	114	395	286	477	768	559
210	621	2142	463	254	415	416	577	858	909
390	671		503	(704)	1805	616	757	1488	1679
410	1071		693	804	1895	2136	1117	(668)	1909
730	1191		893	1754		2356	1667	1998	2139
1030	1231		1063	1874			1997	2048	
2240	2621		1113					2238	
			2033						

Fig 10 'Uniterm' cards

more efficiently by observing the points on the stack at which light is permitted to pass through by virtue of the fact that punchings in the stack coincide. Figure 11 illustrates the principle. Punching positions represent document numbers and relevant documents are thus identified. Again, it is obvious that with these systems we can concern ourselves with only those combinations which we choose to use for search by simply selecting the appropriate feature cards and searching for common numbers by one method or the other. The great virtue of such systems is that they eliminate the need to pass the whole file through the searching device. A disadvantage is that it is not usually possible to store a copy of the document or an abstract in the file, and it is necessary to refer to a separate register to determine the identity of relevant documents. With item entry systems it is possible

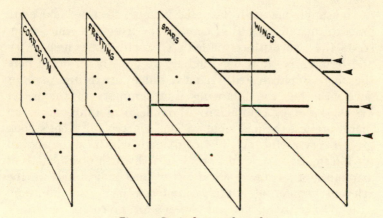

Fig 11 Optical stencil cards

to attach the document identity, and more, to the indexing vehicle, e.g. an abstract can be printed on a hand-sorted or machine-sorted card.

Francis Bello, writing in *Fortune* on the information retrieval problem stated: 'Taube's Uniterms are simply the significant terms, or keywords, in a document. If a document contains ten Uniterms it must be indexed under each of them. Each Uniterm is given its own file card or equivalent (producing a so-called "inverted" file). It is this multiple indexing, primarily, that distinguishes Taube's system from an ordinary office filing system in which one copy of a document or letter is filed under the single heading deemed to be most appropriate'.[4] That Taube's system differs from an office system in that it has multiple entry instead of single entry is undoubtedly true, but this statement is one of the many which completely miss the point, for in this particular concept Uniterm does not differ from conventional library indexes which have multiple entry. What is so important is that some of the multiple entries can be searched simultaneously, on the mathematical 'combination' principle and it is here that a co-ordinate system scores, because neither an office filing system nor a conventional library index can do this.

The simple manually operated systems described above are practical manifestations of co-ordinate principles and demonstrate the two distinct methods of application: item entry and term entry. It is not intended to describe in detail here the more sophisticated systems which are being used or developed, but the following is a summary of the better known types of equipment. More detailed information on 'hardware' can be had from various sources and Kent's book gives a very useful review of equipment which can be applied for information retrieval purposes.[5] Ashworth gives details of a number of specific applications of 'mechanical aids' in the relevant chapter of ASLIB's *Handbook of special librarianship*.[6] Other useful general surveys are given in the article in *Fortune* mentioned above and in *Chemical and Engineering News*.[7]

Of item entry systems, the best known, apart from hand-sorted punched cards, is perhaps the sequential scanning of machine-sorted punched cards. An orthodox punched-card sorter can be used for this purpose, and adaptations which convert the machine to a 'group selection sorter' permit more economical searching by scanning several columns at a time. This seems to be an obvious application of punched card machinery for retrieval purposes, but in fact, in spite of high machine speeds the operation is fairly slow, card wear can be a problem, and the great disadvantage of having to pass the whole file through the machine for each search militates strongly against its use.

Other kinds of individual item unit have been developed

such as the Eastman Kodak 'Minicard'. Here the unit is a piece of film no larger than 0·6″ × 1·3″ which bears both coded indexing information and a microreproduction of the document or its abstract. Coding is carried out by punching into paper tape and conversion from the tape to the film. Searching is a similar process to that of searching machine-sorted punched cards, but is done photo-electrically. Selected cards can be viewed by magnification in a reader. Minicards are stored in 'sticks', each of which will hold about 2,000. This facilitates breaking up the store by subject, date, etc., and searching time is reduced by feeding only those sticks which are relevant, to the machine. Sorting speed is about 1,800 cards a minute.

A similar system to Minicards is the 'Filmorex' system developed by Dr Samain in France. The microfilm cards in this system are 1·4″ × 2·4″. Coding is carried out by the use of a set of 'vocabulary cards' each of which bears black squares along one edge. Cards are selected according to the codings assigned to the document by the indexer and overlapping the cards produces a mosaic representing the document's overall subject content. This mosaic is then transferred photographically along with the document or its abstract, in microform, on to the film.

Another system using separate item entry units is the 'Filmsort' system marketed by Minnesota Mining and Manufacturing Co. This uses punched cards which can be manipulated by ordinary punched card machinery, but each card has an aperture which bears a microfilm of the document. Sorting and selection is by conventional punched card machine procedures. This method is being used by some organisations for storing engineering drawings.

A number of other sophisticated item entry systems store their records not in separate units but in continuous form. One of the best known systems of this kind is the 'Rapid Selector' devised by Dr Vannevar Bush and further developed by Dr Ralph Shaw. The store here consists of reels of 35 mm microfilm which bears a micro-image of each document and appropriate subject coding. When a search is made the machine is set to search the films photo-electrically and when a match is found between search designation and code on the film, a copy of the relevant document is printed automatically, without any stopping or slowing of the film. There are two commercial systems using reels of film in this way, one marketed by Benson-Lehner under the name FLIP and the other by FMA Inc under the name FILESEARCH,

It is also possible to use this principle with either magnetic tape or punched paper tape in conjunction with a computer, or a special device. There is no accompanying microreproduction of the document with the indexing code, but it is possible to provide for recording either a document identity number or any manageable amount of text such as an abstract. The Western Reserve University Searching Selector uses a punched paper tape, with its coding in the form of a 'telegraphic abstract'. This is a machine designed specifically for information retrieval purposes, though it has recently been replaced at Western Reserve University by a General Electric GE 225 computer.

Term entry systems have not been subjected to mechanisation to the same extent as item entry systems. There are only two principle forms in which such mechanisation has taken place: comparison of lists of document numbers on magnetic tapes used with computers, and collation of machine sorted cards. Perhaps a major consideration here has been the fact that it is not easy or economic to store a copy of a document or its abstract with the indexing record because the record appears in several places, determined by the number of terms which have been assigned to the document. When magnetic tapes are used the procedure consists of selecting those lengths of tape which list the document numbers under the terms selected for search and running the tapes through the computer to seek numbers which are common to the several terms. Other media such as punched paper tape, magnetic discs, etc., could be used, but there does not seem to be much promise in the use of such media in this particular way.

When machine sorted cards are used for term entry systems it is necessary to use one card per term per document. In other words, if we assign to a document twenty indexing terms we must provide twenty separate cards, each bearing an indexing term and the identity number of the document. This seems an extravagant use of cards, but cards are comparatively cheap and the smallest of machine-sorted cards will meet the requirement. The cards are then filed in blocks, one block for each term. When a search is made two of the terms selected for search are dealt with by taking the block of cards for each of the terms and passing the two blocks through a 'collator'. The collator searches for pairs of cards with matching identity numbers and separates these cards from the unmatched cards. The rejects from the two blocks are fed into separate pockets and the matched cards appear as a third merged block, or as two identical matched blocks. The block of cards for the third selected search term is then taken and run against one of the blocks of matched cards and this process repeated until all the search terms have been handled. The resulting matched cards represent documents relevant to the search.

This method forms the basis of the IBM 9900 Special Index Analyzer (COMAC), a collator designed to manipulate the blocks of cards in a way best suited to the special requirements of this system. The output from this machine is punched into paper tape, thus giving a listing of relevant document numbers. It is obvious that one advantage of this system is the ease with which up-dating can be carried out, for all that is necessary is to add newly-produced cards for new documents to the existing blocks.

There are other machines being developed to assist in the problem of information retrieval which consist solely of sophisticated document stores, all based on a high degree of micro-miniaturisation with facilities for recovering given items by citing their addresses, but with no provision for coding by subject. These systems, which include AVCO Corporation's VERAC and IBM's PROJECT WALNUT are document stores rather than retrieval machines and are therefore outside the scope of this book. Other devices such as IBM's RAMAC, which have 'random access' facility are also not relevant to our subject here, for they have no apparent virtue other than the possible mechanisation of a process analogous to conventional catalogue consultation. The problem of the economics of storing document images with the indexing information and the general question of the physical nature of the equipment used are matters to be settled within the contexts of particular projected installations. Taube has discussed the question of relative costs of stores with and without text records and coding combined.[8]

Before leaving the question of equipment and possible methods of application of co-ordinate indexing, mention ought to be made of what seems to be a unique approach in that it is the only attempt to provide for visual sequential scanning of item entry records. This is the 'scan-column index' described by O'Connor, which consists of sheets ruled into vertical columns, with provision for posting to these columns symbols representing the various terms assigned to a document.[9] Each document entry occupies one horizontal line and the columns are 'scanned' vertically to detect those entries having the combination of terms specified for search. O'Connor has even put forward a proposal for attaching such an index in roll form to a microfilm reader, with synchronisation between the roll and the microfilm reels, so that when a relevant document is seen in the index, an image of the document is seen on the reader because turning the index roll to reveal this entry has automatically positioned the microfilm for viewing.[10] The scan-column index seems to provide a very laborious method of searching but it is interesting in that it emphasises that what is being sought for information retrieval purposes is something which facilitates 'combination' searching, for this is exactly what the method does.

Our concern in this chapter has been to show the ways in which the solution to the problems of providing flexibility in 'combination' searching can be achieved, and to outline briefly the kinds of equipment which can be brought to bear on the problems. Of the two basic principles of item entry and term entry, the latter has much to commend it and it is currently being applied very successfully by using the beautifully simple and effective optical stencil card method. The very largest organisations may be able to justify the use of costly equipment, but even here the practicability of item entry systems is open to doubt on account of the need to pass the whole file through the machine every time a search is made. For a very large number of organisations, the simpler equipment, at negligible cost, using the term entry principle, seems likely to be favoured for some time to come.

REFERENCES

1 Lee, H. N. *Symbolic logic: an introductory textbook for non-mathematicians*, Routledge, London, 1962, p. 65.

2 McCormick, E. M. Why computers? In The American University, Center for Technology and Administration, *Machine indexing: progress and problems. Papers presented at the Third Institute on Information Storage and Retrieval, 13th–17th February 1961*, pp. 220-32.

3 Jahoda, G. *Correlative indexing systems for the control of research records*. Columbia University, D.L.S. thesis, 1960. University Microfilms Mic 60-3082, p. 31.

4 Bello, F. How to cope with information. *Fortune*, Vol. LXII, No. 3, September 1960, pp. 162-7, 180, 182, 187, 189, 192.

5 Kent, A. *Textbook on mechanized information retrieval*, Interscience, New York, 1962.

6 Ashworth, W. A review of mechanical aids in library work. In *Handbook of special librarianship and information work*, edited by W. Ashworth, 2nd edition, ASLIB, London, 1962, pp. 401-35.

7 Information Retrieval, *Chemical and Engineering News*, Vol. 39, No. 29, 17th July 1961, pp. 102-14.

8 Taube, M. Documentation, information retrieval and other new techniques. *Library Quarterly*, Vol. 31, No. 1, January 1961, pp. 90-103.

9 O'Connor, J. The Scan-column Index. *American Documentation*, Vol. 13, No. 2, April 1962, pp. 204-9.

10   O'Connor, J. A possibly inexpensive attachment for a microfilm reader to permit synchronized co-ordinate searching. *Journal of Chemical Documentation*, Vol. 3, No. 1, January 1963, pp. 29-32.

6

The Control of Indexing Language

The problem of terminology and its control has been with us since the indexing and classification of information began. It forms a major part of the subjects discussed in chapters 2 and 3 and is undoubtedly the greatest barrier to progress in solving the information retrieval problem. The manipulation of subject concepts in retrieval systems, once they are properly labelled, is not a difficult thing to manage and it is evident from the foregoing chapters that the mechanics of such manipulation is susceptible to effective control and useful application. Conventional systems achieved their purpose satisfactorily when conditions were such that subject designations demanded no more than they were able to provide, and since the complexity of subjects has outstripped their capabilities the newer techniques of co-ordinate indexing have provided us with all that is necessary to redress the balance in this particular respect.

We must be careful, however, to distinguish between what a system is capable of doing with regard to accepting, storing, and subsequently manipulating pieces of information which are labelled unmistakably and unambiguously in the system's special language once the information is in the system, and the problem of designating the subject both for indexing and searching purposes *before* this manipulation takes place. The former is a question of 'information theory' which is concerned with the efficiency and economics of conveying 'bits' of information, but information of a special kind. A useful distinction between this information and information in the sense in which we think of it for storage and retrieval purposes is made in Hughes' *Electronic engineer's reference book*: 'Information in a certain sense is now recognised to be a measurable quantity. In contrast to the aspect of information concerned with the abstract idea of meaning or sense, which is called *semantic* information, that which is measurable in engineering terms may be called *selective* information.'[1] When we speak of 'information theory' we are talking of 'selective information'. When we speak of indexing language for information retrieval we are talking of 'semantic information'.

It is sometimes argued that we should concern ourselves with information theory only, for if we become involved in 'meaning' or 'semantics' we are inviting trouble. This view is very hard to understand on two counts. Firstly both the input and output of retrieval systems are concerned with subjects stated in ordinary language and we must at some stage in each case be concerned with the meaning of the terms used. Secondly we have not yet demanded from communication engineers solutions to problems which present any real difficulty, nor is there any indication that we are likely to do so. Information theory is likely to be more than a match for any difficulties which information retrieval throws up in the foreseeable future. The real difficulty is that of designating subjects properly in the first place so that a designation can be matched whatever approach is made to the system when the document concerned will be useful to the searcher. Once this problem has been mastered there is not likely to be any difficulty in arranging for the indexing language to be handled efficiently by the system, whether ordinary language terms are used or a code is adopted. As far as the more sophisticated machines are concerned problems of information theory are not likely to limit the use of the indexing language.

Conventional systems use terms in ordinary language either in the main file, as with the alphabetical subject catalogue or in the index to the main file, as with the classified catalogue. No great difficulty is met with in such systems as far as the meaning of a statement of a subject in words is concerned, for the usual features of ordinary language such as the adjectival or participial forms of words normally show what the meaning is intended to be. This is not to say, of course, that there are no semantic problems but in such systems all the terms designating a subject are found together in the form of a subject heading or an index entry and factors such as syntax and context ensure that the intended meaning is clearly conveyed. When non-conventional systems are considered however, a new problem arises and this is that the various elements in a subject designation, i.e. the individual terms, must be dealt with separately in the retrieval operation. They may not be physically separated, in that with item entry systems they will appear on the same entry, but the searcher is likely to instruct the system to search for only some of the terms concerned and an ordinary statement of the subject cannot meet this sort of requirement because the searcher does not state it or 'read' it as a whole and context cannot therefore be effective.

This problem can be separated into two distinct parts: (a) the indication of which individual terms are to be linked into groups to form subject designations, and (b) the function of the thing represented by each such term in the designation. The first of these can be solved by what Vickery refers to as 'interlocking descriptors'[2] but there are really two different kinds of interlocking required. To illustrate the two kinds let us take the case of a document whose main subject is the friction of yarns on knitting machines as affected by the surfaces of yarn guides but which deals with two subsidiary subjects which were relevant to the investigation: the development of a special device for measuring yarn tension and the effect of relative humidity on the tension of yarn being drawn off bobbins. We might assign the following terms to this document in indexing: FRICTION, YARNS, KNITTING, SURFACES, GUIDES, TENSIOMETERS, HUMIDITY, TENSION, TAKE-OFF, BOBBINS. Suppose that an enquirer is seeking information on errors in tensiometers as affected by the friction of their moving parts and in interrogating the system cites the terms FRICTION and TENSIOMETERS. This document will be retrieved because these two terms were assigned in indexing but it probably has no information on this subject.

There is a very simple solution to this problem and that is to regard the three separate subjects as being three separate documents and to assign to each such 'unit of information' a separate identity number. It is then impossible to have 'false co-ordinations' of this kind. This must be done with discretion of course, for if the second of the subsidiary subjects in this case was directly connected with the main subject, i.e. the document dealt with the way in which the effect of relative humidity on the take-off tension from bobbins affected friction of yarns on knitting machines, then the enquirer is entitled to expect to retrieve this document when he asks for this subject, and separate numbers should not be assigned.

Suppose, however, that the three subjects are quite separate and that we assign the three numbers 7369, 7370 and 7371 to the document to designate the respective subjects. We have now introduced the first kind of interlocking and the several terms of the main subject are interlocked by virtue of the fact that the number 7369 has been assigned to each. Suppose now that the enquirer requests information on the friction of yarns on knitting machines as affected by the surface of the yarn itself. (Both the subject of this document and the subject of this enquiry are perfectly realistic examples of problems in the textile field.) If he cites the terms FRICTION, YARNS, KNITTING, SURFACES the document will again be retrieved but will be irrelevant. This problem is not so easily solved because we cannot do any further separating into smaller units as each subject unit must be preserved as an entity and must be retrieved if specified as such. The basic number must be preserved in order to ensure matching when com-bination of any or all terms in the designation is used in searching.

This difficulty can be overcome by taking the basic number 7369, and adding to it something which will qualify it, this something being common to the several postings to the terms to be interlocked. Perhaps the simplest type of qualifier is a further digit added after a decimal point, but this can be used only in those cases where numbers are posted as numbers and are not designated by position as with optical stencil cards. This method could be used, for instance in a system using Uniterm cards and the postings could be:

YARNS	7369
FRICTION	7369
SURFACES	7369·1
KNITTING	7369
GUIDES	7369·1

When a search is made with a system such as this it is necessary for the searcher to consider his list of search terms and
anticipate false combinations. He then selects those terms
which he sees must be linked and does a preliminary search on
any such group. If he finds that a group whose terms he has
stated must be interlocked does not give a match of basic
number plus modifier, then there is no point in pursuing the
search further. An alternative method is to search all terms
for matching basic numbers and to do a final check for matching modifiers on the numbers so produced.

With optical stencil card systems a number is determined
by the position of a hole. Changing the position of a hole
changes the number, but there is one course left open to us
and that is to leave the hole where it is but to change its
shape. Thus the standard hole could be round and if a first
qualifier were required a triangular hole could be used, if a
second pair (or more) of terms needed to be linked a square
hole could be used and so on. In the list of terms above, all
would be punched in the position 7369 but YARNS, FRICTION
and KNITTING would have round holes whilst SURFACES and
GUIDES would have triangular ones. Stacking of any or all of
the cards would show coincidence, but a search for information on yarn surfaces would produce coincidence of a round
with a triangular hole and the irrelevance of this document
would be evident. It is very doubtful whether these refinements are worth the trouble as final sorting for 'false drops'
after a search in a system without them is unlikely to be much
more than a few minutes work, but there may be cases where
special circumstances justify their incorporation and these
examples of application to the simpler manual systems
illustrate the principles involved.

The modifications discussed above are known as 'links' and

a simple description of their use is given in an article by Morse.[3] The links described by Morse are applied by the addition of decimals to the main numbers but their use is confined to distinguishing between subject units, and does not extend to the linking of terms within units.

When we have isolated subject units and indicated by the use of links which terms are related to each other within such units, there may still be ambiguity because the concepts represented by the grouped terms within the units have particular 'roles' which are clearly defined in the ordinary language statement of the subject but which are not apparent from the mere listing and linking of terms for entry into the retrieval system. An example will make this clear. Suppose we have a subject unit which deals with the reaction between ethylene and water to produce ethanol, using phosphoric acid as catalyst. When indexing this information we should enter into the system the terms ETHYLENE, WATER, ETHANOL and PHOSPHORIC ACID. We may also have information on the reaction which produces ethylene and water from ethanol, using activated alumina as catalyst. Clearly, the same terms will be entered into the system for this subject as for the first one, with the exception of the term for the catalyst which will be ALUMINA instead of PHOSPHORIC ACID. Now if we search for information on the production of ethanol from ethylene and water, without citing the catalyst, both these documents will be retrieved, but the second one will be irrelevant. We can do no more by the use of interlocking, but we can introduce another kind of qualifier in order to remove this ambiguity. The modification in this case is to the term itself and not to the document identity as it is with interlocking.

The meaning of an individual term must not be changed, of course, but the variable in cases of this sort is the function of the thing represented by the term in the particular activity which is the subject of a document. Thus, in the first case above the function or 'role' of the ethylene is that of a starting material, as is that of the water, but the role of the ethanol is that of product. Similarly the role of the phosphoric acid is that of catalyst. In order to provide for this refinement in a given subject field it is necessary to determine the total number of such roles in which terms might operate. Having created the list of roles, each term in the vocabulary is considered in relation to the list in order to determine which roles it may assume in various situations. Thus some documents may deal with phosphoric acid as a starting material, some as a product, some as a catalyst, some as a drying agent, some as an inhibitor, etc. If these five roles were considered to be pertinent to the given subject field, then phosphoric acid would be considered to be five separate terms and if a Uniterm or optical stencil card system were in use for instance, then there would be separate cards for:

> Phosphoric acid (starting material)
> Phosphoric acid (product)
> Phosphoric acid (catalyst)
> Phosphoric acid (drying agent)
> Phosphoric acid (inhibitor)

Proper selection of cards for search would then prevent ambiguity of the kind discussed above. These qualifiers are known as 'role indicators' and the article by Morse referred to above deals also with these devices, though an associated article by Holm[4] covers the principle more fully and lists the ten roles lettered A–J, which have since been used in the indexing of journals published by the American Institute of Chemical Engineers. Each article in these journals now carries indexing terms with appropriate links and roles.

Another way in which the 'roles' of terms can be considered is that of 'categorisation'. The roles assigned to phosphoric acid above might be regarded as the names of categories to which terms in a subject field might be assigned and it is sometimes possible so to organise a field that everything which is stated as the subject of a document can be stated in a standard form. If, for instance we are concerned with reports on the testing of certain components, the number of features which are significant may be quite small, with each such feature

forming a well-defined 'category'. Our features here may be:
(1) the component concerned (2) material of which made (3)
type of construction, e.g. rivetted, welded, bonded, etc. (4)
temperature at which test carried out, and (5) kind of test,
e.g. fatigue, tension, compression, bending, etc. This categorisation is adopted on the assumption that all tests can be
reported by citing one term in each of the categories, e.g.
fatigue tests at high temperatures on rivetted aluminium
plates. An obvious application of this principle is the use of
machine-sorted punched cards, with a 'field' allocated to each
category on the card layout, because searching such 'fixed'
fields, with a comparatively limited vocabulary is a very
positive and efficient method of retrieval. A good example
of such an application is that described by Patterson, Ackley
and Rehmeyer,[5] which was designed for use in the pharma-
ceutical field. Here the main categories are but three in
number, i.e. biological terms, which represent such things as
conditions to be treated by drugs, 'major verbs', which
represent the activity linking the first and third categories,
such as 'treated with', 'decreased by', etc., and chemical terms
representing compounds affecting the things represented by
the terms in the first category. These are considerably
elaborated by provision for 'modulants' and 'minor verbs' but
the basic structure of the three categories referred to as
'subject', 'major verb' and 'effector' is preserved and though
several machine-sorted cards are used for each subject, fixed
fields and a fixed order of cards are used and there is therefore
positive control. There are, of course, disadvantages to the
use of sequential scanning of machine-sorted cards and this is
not suggested as necessarily being the best way to apply the
principle of categorisation. Indeed this article describes the
special provision which was made for feeding the content of
the cards to a computer for manipulation therein.

Another very interesting example of categorisation, with a
rather different mode of application, is the principle on which
the experimental American Chemical Society publication
Chemical-Biological Activities, is based. This publication, of
which a sample issue was produced with the date September

1962, was conceived as 'an index to current literature on the biological activity of organic compounds'. The information is prepared for input to the system by 'document analysts' and this, the raw material for index entries, is then manipulated by a computer which writes out the information in sentences of the standard form 'Compound A has action B on system C', and this it does by reference to a dictionary tape. A Keyword-in-Context index by names of compounds and significant terms is then prepared from these sentences, together with molecular formula, notation, and author indexes. Three basic categories are thus recognised: the biological system acted upon (C), the compound performing the action (A) and the type of action (B) and it will be noticed that there is a remarkable similarity between these categories and those used in the punched-card system described above. In the latter case, of course, the categories were tied to fixed fields on the cards, but their purpose here is nevertheless similar in that they establish a standard form for the statement of a subject in the system, so that matching in searching is a positive process. The fact that the one system provides for co-ordinate searches in the several fields whilst the other provides for the production of a printed index for searching under single terms does not alter the fact that categorisation has been introduced to help control the indexing language.

The categorisation discussed here implies that we are concerned with a very small number of categories and within a given subject field it is often possible to meet requirements by such provision because subject designations lend themselves to formulation by the use of such a small number. The place of a term is always clear because subject designations reflect a standard and oft-repeated activity such as those of component testing and biological investigations. But the categories here are very special ones in that it is only the special context which places a term in a given category. A 'plate' belongs to the category of 'subject of test' only because it is being considered in a testing context. It has no inherent relationship to such a category. It is, unfortunately, not always possible to state subject designations in this highly

E

formalised way and Fairthorne stated this very clearly when, talking of documentation of information on drugs in the USA, he said 'For here a very strict form of query is put to the system; that is, what treatment? what condition? and what results? When you have highly standardised queries of that sort of course the various freak methods and mechanical methods are liable to be more successful than in some other fields. Also, chemistry is—relatively speaking—highly disciplined in its terminology compared with some other activities. Actually it is rather unfortunate that most non-conventional documentation on a big scale originated in the field of chemistry. People have got the idea that other activities can be so highly structured and highly systematised as chemistry can be. They are wrong'.[6]

For those circumstances in which it is not possible to reduce subject designations to such well defined forms, we must make other kinds of provision for the control of the indexing language. Categorisation of some kind enters into such provision in most cases, but the kinds of categorisation produce different kinds of vocabulary. The most rigorous application is that to be found in faceted classification schemes for faceted schedules are produced on the very principle of categorisation, with careful attention to the principles of applying a single characteristic for the production of one category. Vickery states the principle thus: 'Facet analysis, by means of fundamental distinguishing characteristics or categories, is the basic operation in constructing a faceted classification.'[7] The significant point about this is that the terms in a category so produced are mutually exclusive and it is therefore impossible to find more than one term in the category which will meet a given situation. It is not so easy in practice to produce groups of such mutually exclusive terms because of the nature of language, but it is easier in some cases than in others. We might take as an example of a category the group of terms representing 'engineering operations' which would form part of a simple classification of aeronautics, and though it may be argued that these are not strictly mutually exclusive, they are reasonably so:

Design
Development
Assembly
Testing
Servicing

Facet analysis, therefore, sets out to produce lists of mutually exclusive terms and because of its ability to do this it is a powerful tool for retrieval purposes. Its usefulness may, in the final analysis, prove to lie more in the field of non-conventional techniques than in its application to the production of faceted schedules for use as classification schemes in the orthodox way.

Another kind of categorisation is manifested in that newcomer to the information retrieval field, the 'thesaurus'. We must examine this in detail, for the thesaurus is being accepted as a panacea, without much real understanding of what it tries to do or how well it succeeds. The thesaurus best known to the English-speaking world is that of Peter Mark Roget and its form typifies the general conception of the nature of a thesaurus, i.e. a classified arrangement of words according to the ideas which they express, its purpose being to provide a reference tool for those who, wishing to express a given idea, and having a particular but inadequate word in mind, seek a word which will enable them to express that idea with the maximum effectiveness.

The purpose of a thesaurus is therefore to list against a given term or phrase those terms or phrases which are synonymous or nearly synonymous with it, but the degree to which the listed terms correspond in meaning to the leading term depends on what degree of latitude the thesaurus maker allows himself when considering the eligibility of a particular term for inclusion in a particular group. The problem of deciding how far to go in this respect was summed up by John L. Roget, editor of the 1879 edition of Roget's *Thesaurus* and son of the original compiler: 'Were we, on the other hand, to attempt to include, in each category of the *Thesaurus*, every word and phrase which could by any possibility be appropriately used in relation to the leading idea for which that category was designed, we should impair, if not destroy, the whole use and value of the book. . . . The small cluster of nearly synonymous words, which had formed the nucleus of a category, would be lost in a sea of phrases, and it would be difficult to recognise those which were peculiarly adapted to express the leading ideas.'

It is clear that the kind of grouping of terms which a thesaurus is intended to provide is that which depends on similarity of meaning of the terms. It is important to appreciate that this is quite the reverse of what a faceted arrangement of terms provides, for facet analysis sets out to ensure that the terms in a category are different to the extent of their being mutually exclusive. A thesaurus sets out to provide lists of terms which can be substituted one for another, whereas the possibility of substitution of one term for another within a category of a faceted arrangement is the surest evidence that the facet analysis has been faulty. Taking the list of terms comprising the simple category given above, whereas no term can be substituted for another without changing the meaning of a subject designation of which the term forms part, there may be other terms which could serve in place of the scheduled one. Thus, if we take the term 'assembly', we may consider that any of the following terms would serve just as well in its stead :

Construction
Erection
Building

Schedules of mutually exclusive terms such as those provided by facet analysis should provide us with no choice but the right one. Thesauri give us a great deal of choice, for provision of choice is their very purpose. A group of terms from which a choice can be made should be regarded as a single focus in the appropriate facet, real or imaginary, of a faceted schedule, and choice between foci is, by definition, impossible.

This distinction is important, because the purpose and mode of use of thesauri has not been clearly defined and several different kinds can be recognised. Vickery[8] has examined a number of thesauri and deals with those compiled by Luhn, Bernier and Heumann, Heald, and Wall. We need not consider here the detailed analysis which Vickery makes, but a clear distinction must be made between two different appreciations of what a thesaurus is which have grown up since the idea was first introduced into the retrieval field. One is that a thesaurus is what Roget intended it to be, i.e. a list of alternatives to be used at will. The other is that it groups terms, not for the purpose of providing acceptable alternatives, but for the specific purpose of prohibiting the use of alternatives, there being a standard term which is to be used whenever it or any of the terms in the group arises, either in indexing or searching. Of the first kind, the thesaurus issued by the American Institute of Chemical Engineers[9] is a well known example, but neither the work itself nor the two articles which introduced it (those by Morse and Holm cited above) make it clear how the thesaurus is to be used, though there is a clear explanation in these two papers of the mechanics of operating a co-ordinate system. Let us consider the effect of using a thesaurus of this type.

We are accustomed to the principle of suggestion of alternative terms in retrieval systems in the form of 'see also' references ('see' references are not suggestions, but instructions) and the simple alphabetical subject catalogue is the best known type of system using such references. If we proceed through all the necessary steps in making a search in an alphabetical subject catalogue we can exhaust every possibility within the limits of the quality of the catalogue and conclude with reasonable certainty that we have not missed any relevant item which the catalogue includes. This is because we examine in turn all those headings which are likely to include entries for relevant documents, being guided in this by the 'see alsos', and perhaps in the first place being directed by a 'see' reference.

When we are concerned with complex subjects and adopt a co-ordinate system because of this complexity, we abandon the principle of searching under one subject heading at a time and adopt the procedure of searching with several terms simultaneously. With the former we can methodically pass from one heading to another until we have examined every potentially fruitful entry, but if we try to do the same thing with the several terms involved in a search in a co-ordinate system we can run into real difficulty. Suppose we have in the vocabulary used in a retrieval system for an aeronautical collection the following groups of terms:

Wings	Delta	Interference	Speed	Scoops	Calculation
Aerofoils	Triangular		Mach	Inlets	Estimation
Lifting	Dart-		number	Intakes	Determination
surfaces	shaped				

If we search for information on 'the estimation of the effect of Mach number on the interference between scoops and triangular aerofoils', we are faced with the possibility of using any one term in each of these groups when choosing our six terms for search because each group can be considered to be a set of synonymous or nearly synonymous terms. As we have 3 terms in the first group, 3 in the second, 1 in the third, 2 in the fourth, 3 in the fifth and 3 in the sixth, the total number of possible combinations of terms to use in searching is $3 \times 3 \times 1 \times 2 \times 3 \times 3 = 162$. This means that with a Uniterm system or optical stencil cards we should have to take 162 different combinations of cards and carry out the search with each such separate set! This, of course, is an exaggerated case specially designed to illustrate the principle but this problem does arise in practice with thesauri which really are thesauri in the accepted sense.

There is an obvious solution to this problem and that is to use in indexing all the terms from a given category which could possibly be considered to be reasonable search terms. This course is what is known as 'redundant indexing' and Holm and Rasmussen[10] discuss the use of redundancy in either indexing or searching, or both. The thesaurus of the American Institute of Chemical Engineers is based on that compiled at E. I. du Pont de Nemours & Co of which company's staff these authors are members, and the policy of du Pont, which is stated in this article, is to index redundantly.

It is clear from the indexing information provided with articles in A.I.Ch.E. publications, such as *Chemical Engineering Progress* that redundant indexing is carried out here also. Whilst it is possible to find cases here of possible failure in recall because of the alternative terms available, most cases seem to be catered for by redundancy in assigning terms. As far as redundancy in searching is concerned, it is clearly impracticable to do this in manual systems, as demonstrated above, but it can be done in computer systems of course by programming the machine to search with a very large number of alternative questions.

The purpose of redundant indexing is to increase the probability of success in retrieval, or in other words to increase recall factor. The inevitable result of this, with a given vocabulary, is to reduce the pertinency factor and there is evidence of this effect of redundant indexing. Jaster, Murray and Taube discuss the experience of indexing in the Man-Machine Information Center of Documentation Incorporated and state 'The M-MIC personnel frequently found that over indexing contributed to the retrieval of excess material.'[11] This interdependence between recall factor and pertinency factor is bound to exist with a given vocabulary but we should not accept that we are left with no course other than to select that particular balance between recall and pertinency which suits our requirements best. This point is fundamental for it is vocabulary quality which determines the level of recall and pertinence and an increase of quality will push one up without depressing the other, or better still, will increase both. Careful attention to choice of terms and their 'control' should have this effect and the considerable amount of research now being carried out may in due course produce refinements which increase efficiency in terms of both recall and pertinence to a level much higher than that at which we must operate currently. The word 'control' is often used to denote the purpose of thesauri, but the kind of thesaurus discussed above can hardly be claimed to control terminology. It simply provides masses of alternative terms so that by a process of saturation we can ensure an acceptably high level of recall with possibly disastrous results as far as pertinency is concerned. Roget provided for choice, which is what his users want. The user of a thesaurus for retrieval purposes wants no choice, but positive instructions with regard to the course which he must take once he has made his initial approach.

The second kind of thesaurus offers a possible solution to this problem for the principle used here is to telescope all the terms in a category into a single term. In other words one term is chosen as the standard term and this is used at all times in place of the alternatives. This is the type of thesaurus proposed by Luhn in connection with the automatic encoding of documents by machine, though Luhn uses a code number for each category rather than a word.[12, 13] This seems to be a very much more realistic approach, for here we have real control in that we either accept a given term for incorporation in the thesaurus, or suppress it in favour of another and as far as the user is concerned, choice, with the possibility of a wrong choice, is eliminated. The important point about this sort of thesaurus is that the wisdom with which terms are accepted or rejected governs its success or failure as a retrieval tool. The trouble is, of course, that terms do not group themselves neatly into mutually exclusive lists so that one can be selected and all the others suppressed. Even when we do have our groupings a decision on whether to telescope the terms will depend on several factors. One of these is the question of how the 'resolving power' of the system, that is the ability of the system to separate out one document from the rest, is affected by the co-ordination of several terms in searching. Thus, whilst we may lump together several terms under a term which serves for them all, the fact that another term in the vocabulary can apply to only one of the several telescoped terms means that when we co-ordinate in searching the resolving power of the system is as good as if all the terms had been listed separately.

If, for instance, we had some aeronautical documents as marginal material in a non-aeronautical collection, we may quite satisfactorily use the term 'aircraft structures' to serve for 'wings', 'undercarriages', and 'fuselages'. If we have additionally the separate terms 'lift', 'drop tests' and 'pressure tests', then if we co-ordinate 'aircraft structures' with 'drop tests' we shall retrieve only documents on drop tests on under-carriages for such tests are not likely to be performed on wings or fuselages. Similarly co-ordination of 'aircraft structures' with 'lift' will produce only documents on lift of wings and its co-ordination with 'pressure tests' will produce only documents on pressure tests of fuselages. Another thing to take into account is that though the resolving power of the system may be high when co-ordination takes place, we may wish to use the system to meet requests for information on things which are in themselves very specific without further qualification, that is by citing the term for a given concept alone, without any co-ordination with other terms. Thus in an aeronautical collection it is reasonable to expect to be able to retrieve all the information there is on 'vortex generators', and to bury this term under a term representing a group of things would be to impair this facility. In the final analysis it seems that the telescoping or opening up of categories of terms in such a thesaurus will depend on the subject field and the operating conditions which are applicable. In some categories a great deal of compression will be possible whilst in others maximum separation will be necessary and each group of terms needs to be judged on the dictates of the particular environment. Luhn cites the example of the word 'butterfly' which, if it occurred in a thesaurus for use with documents dealing with electricity, would be 'relegated to a notional family of broader aspects, such as the notions "insects", "animals", or "living things", depending on the overall frequency of occurrence of such notions'.[14] It seems that in practice it is possible to reduce the number of accepted terms in such a thesaurus to a very small figure for Boyd has stated that his system operates satisfactorily on a vocabulary of as few as 427 terms.[15]

Of the two types of thesaurus distinguished above, only the first type is a thesaurus in the accepted sense and the second might better be called a 'standard word list' or 'authority list'. Subject headings lists for conventional alphabetical subject cataloguing have sometimes been called 'authority lists' and there is very little, if any, difference in principle between such lists and this second type of thesaurus. They differ mainly in that the conventional list accepts compound terms whereas the thesaurus limits itself more to individual words.

In addition to these two principal types of thesaurus there are other less fundamental variations on the theme. The thesaurus discussed by Bernier and Heumann,[16] to which Vickery makes reference, is pictured as derived from a 'vocabulary ball' which has the most specific terms in the subject field forming its surface and the most general lying at its centre, with a gradation from specific to general as we pass from surface to centre. Each 'layer' of terms is related to the next innermost layer by virtue of the fact that its terms are merely one grade less abstract than those of this next layer. We can thus select a particular level of generality of terms by 'peeling' layers from the ball and this level will determine the nature of the resulting thesaurus.

This technique, though it seems highly theoretical, would obviously provide a method of structuring a thesaurus, but the way in which the proposed thesaurus differs from those already mentioned is that the authors suggest that any given term in a given layer can be defined by the relevant terms from the next innermost layer. The term is thus not accepted as a term to be used in the system but has substituted for it what is called a 'composite synonym'. This obviously introduces what we might call 'conventions', i.e. the provision of instructions in the thesaurus to the effect that when a given term appears we shall use, not what is usually provided in a thesaurus, that is a synonym or near synonym for the term, but a group of non-synonymous terms which collectively define it.

Another type of word list (not usually referred to as a thesaurus) is the 'word association list'. This consists of an entry for a given term with a listing of all other terms which have been used in conjunction with it in indexing, and sometimes with the number of times this association has taken place. Such a list might have an entry which appears thus:

BRIDGES

CONCRETE	4
DESIGN	2
FAILURE	1
ROADS	7
STRESSES	13
WINDS	3

This indicates that there were 13 documents indexed to which both 'bridges' and 'stresses' were assigned, 3 to which both 'bridges' and 'winds' were assigned and so on. Here, of course, the intention is not to suggest to the searcher that he uses a listed term instead of that which he turns up in the list, which is the procedure with a thesaurus, but to indicate that he might usefully use his selected term plus a listed term for there will certainly be retrieval because the two terms are known to have been associated in the indexing of the number of documents stated. This type of list is discussed by Jaster, Murray and Taube.[17]

One cannot help but feel uneasy about the introduction of devices such as this, for their purpose is quite different from that of thesauri and lists which standardise terminology. The latter enable the searcher to take each of the terms which he has thought of for co-ordination and check each separately to determine whether it is acceptable. The several terms which comprise his final approved list are not brought into association until he interrogates the retrieval system proper. The word association list on the other hand suggests to him what his chances of retrieval are before he approaches the system, for it shows what co-ordinations are provided for. There seems to be something fundamentally wrong with a situation wherein we have adopted a co-ordinate system because of the clear advantages which it has over conventional systems, which were argued in chapter 5, only to revert back to listing in a visible index the same terms as we shall eventually co-ordinate for search. A word association list attempts to tell us what we want. A thesaurus attempts only to help us find it. There is, however, a very strong feeling that the searcher often needs to have his requirements formulated for him, and it may be that this sort of guidance will have some value.

We are here concerned with word lists of various kinds but we might usefully discuss an interesting principle which is not concerned with word lists but is an aspect of the mechanics of co-ordinate indexing. Its relevance here lies in the fact that it provides the facility discussed above of enabling a searcher to detect what additional terms might usefully be co-ordinated before actual co-ordination with these additional terms takes place. This is the principle of 'extended fields' and it is described in two separate papers by J. L. Jolley.[18, 19] It goes very much further than does the word association list, for the latter does no more than show the terms which might profitably be co-ordinated with the single word against which the suggested terms are listed. Extended fields will indicate further terms which might be used after several terms have already been co-ordinated.

There is an admirable example of the application of extended fields in the system used by Dowty Rotol Ltd and described briefly by Shedden.[20] An outline of the method used here is perhaps the best way of explaining the principle. The system employs standard ICT 80 column punched cards, which are used peek-a-boo fashion and machine sorting does not come into the picture for ordinary operating purposes. Most of the card, i.e. columns 31–80, is used for orthodox punching of document numbers, but a separate field comprising columns 1–22 is reserved as an extended feature field. Each hole position in this field represents a 'feature', i.e. a term from the vocabulary. When a document is indexed the document number is punched into the document number field on the card for each assigned term in the ordinary way. In the extended feature field of each card the appropriate hole is punched for every other term which has been used in indexing the document. When a search is made by stacking cards there may be a large number of coincident holes in the document field representing far more documents than can conveniently be pulled from the file for examination. There may, however, also be coincident holes in the extended feature field and each such hole represents a term which might profitably be used to narrow down the search and reduce the number of retrieved documents. The searcher is thus able to choose an additional term or terms for co-ordination and to extract the relevant card or cards for stacking. To take a hypothetical example (not from the Dowty Rotol vocabulary) suppose we search for information on the corrosion of cylinder liners in internal combustion engines using the terms CORROSION, CYLINDERS, LINERS, and find on stacking the cards that there is an excess of document numbers revealed. There might also be revealed in the extended field holes representing ACIDS, ELECTROLYTIC and several different kinds of STEEL. This enables the searcher to decide whether he will confine his study to those documents which deal with the effect of acids or electrolytic action on corrosion, or the resistance of different kinds of material. If he chooses to study the effect of acids then he extracts the card for acids and expects that stacking will reduce the number of coincident holes in the document number field. It should be noted that the promise of successful co-ordination made by an extended feature field should not be taken as a certainty for it is possible to produce coincidence of holes in two or more cards by mutual co-ordination in indexing with another term. Such a case can thus produce a blank sort in spite of the indication given by the extended feature field. The fact that this can happen does not invalidate the method as a useful guide. (The article by Shedden also explains how the obvious limitations of capacity of conventional machine sorted cards can be overcome for the use of such cards as an optical stencil system.)

We have so far discussed some aspects of the selection of terms for inclusion in a vocabulary and the control and manipulation of such terms in retrieval systems. We have assumed that it is clearly understood what kinds of subject designation are to be stored in the system, and this is a fair assumption as far as conventional systems are concerned for here we have been accustomed to using terms as we find them, that is we have taken the word or words representing what a thing is usually called and used the expression, suitably standardised, for subject headings in the alphabetical subject catalogue and for entries in the index to the classified catalogue. But we do not have to use the name of a thing in order to record it in a system for we have the alternative course of using a definition of the thing. Typical of this method is the use of 'semantic factoring' by the Center for Documentation, School of Library Science, Western Reserve University,[21, 22] by which a clock is defined as being 'a device for measuring time'. (The significance of definition by semantic factors tends to be lost in the discussions of the very special coding used by Western Reserve, but we are here concerned with the semantic aspect of subject description, and not with coding, which is merely a vehicle for it.)

We might consider the subject of our discussion here as being the question of whether we should think of things as 'what they are or what they are called', in other words is a thermometer 'a device for measuring temperature' or 'a thermometer'? A thing usually has one accepted name, or if there are alternative names they are easily looked after by selecting one as standard and referring from the others as synonyms. There can, however, be different kinds of definition of a thing and one may be appropriate in one set of circumstances, whereas another may serve another purpose best. The attributes which a thing possesses are used to define that thing, but attributes which are not in themselves sufficient for definition are often useful as 'handles' for retrieval purposes, and in this connection it is convenient to talk about the 'intension' of terms for the several kinds of intension cover the several kinds of subject designation which we may wish to use in a retrieval system. There are three such kinds of intension, which are admirably described by Cohen and Nagel:[23]

'1   The intension of a term is sometimes taken to mean the sum total of the attributes which are present to the mind of any person employing the term. Thus to one person the term "robber" signifies: "taking property not lawfully his, socially undesirable, violent," and so forth; to another person it may signify: "taking property with value greater than ten dollars not lawfully his, physically dangerous person, the result of bad disposition," and so on. The intension of a term so understood is called the subjective intension. The subjective intension varies from person to person, and is of psychological rather than of logical significance.

'2 The intension of a term may signify the set of attributes which are essential to it. And by "essential" we mean the necessary and sufficient condition for regarding any object as an element of the term. This condition is generally selected by some convention, so that intension in this sense is called conventional intension or connotation. The conventional intension of a term, as we shall see later, constitutes its definition.

'3 The intension of a term may signify all the attributes which the objects in the denotation of a term have in common, whether these attributes are known or not. This is called the objective intension or comprehension. Thus, if the conventional intension of "Euclidean triangle" is "a plane figure bounded by three straight lines," a part of the objective intension is: "a plane figure with three angles, a plane figure whose angle sum is two right angles," and so on.'

Now if we follow traditional practice, we shall involve ourselves in no more difficulty in the use of terms than are inherent in the problem of ensuring that a subject is always called by the same name. This is difficult enough, of course, and when applied satisfactorily the principle is limited to enabling us to retrieve information on a subject by its usual name. If we wish to retrieve information on something because it possesses a particular attribute, and supposing that the thing is entered only under its usual name, we can retrieve relevant information only by knowing before interrogating the system that the thing about which we seek information possesses that attribute.

When we move away from the conventional system using

'known names' for subjects, we begin to see manifestations
of the three types of intension listed above. The subjects of
the documents comprising a special collection have, in many
cases, interest to the clientele only because of their having a
special application to the activity with which the organisation
is concerned. The chemical substance HYDROGEN PEROXIDE
may be of interest to the textile technologist only because
of the fact that it is known to be useful as a bleaching agent
so the retrieval system for an organisation in the textile field
may, in addition to entry under the name of the substance,
provide an entry under BLEACHING AGENTS, so that a search
for bleaching agents will retrieve information on this substance. Similarly, in the field of rocketry we may find hydrogen
peroxide entered under the heading FUELS, but not, of course,
under BLEACHING AGENTS. If we think of subjective intension
as varying from one group of people to another (i.e. between
the groups of users of different special libraries) rather than
between individuals as stated by Cohen and Nagel, the expression fits this situation perfectly.

The second type of intension, i.e. 'conventional intension'
is the same thing as the definition of a term, and some retrieval
systems encode the subjects of documents in the form of
definitions of the subjects rather than by their names. The
definition of a subject is here taken to be that definition which
best suits the need of the particular system and not necessarily
the standard definition as given in a reference book, though of
course the two will often coincide. Several different definitions
might legitimately be encoded into a single system. The best-
known example of such subject designation is that of Western
Reserve University, which has already been mentioned. A
useful example of the coding used here is that used for
'diamond', which is cited by Jaster, Murray and Taube.[24] They
intimate that the coding for diamond may represent 'a
crystalline form composed of carbon and characterised by
hardness', or where the system requirements are different the
definition might be 'a mineral in crystalline form composed
of carbon and used as a gem'. The purpose of recording subjects in forms such as this, is of course to facilitate searching

not merely by the name 'diamond', but by the semantic factors 'things composed of carbon', 'hard things', 'crystalline forms', 'minerals' or 'gems'. This is the kind of searching discussed in chapter 2 when the universal use of the expression 'generic encoding' was criticised.

The third type of intension is manifested in those systems which endeavour to provide for retrieval by any attribute which a thing may possess. Few systems in practice attempt such ambitious provision, but any future national information service which attempts to provide deep indexing with a view to providing all things for all men will have to travel to some extent at least along this road. We can hardly claim to have scratched the surface of this problem, but it is a very real and fundamental one. Suppose that documents on 'fibrescopes' are entered in such a system and that such devices may be of interest to a variety of the system's users. One enquirer may request information by citing the term FIBRESCOPES because he knows that this is the usual name for the devices. Another may be concerned with the medical field, and knowing that the principle has been applied by passing a bundle of fibres through a vein for the purpose of examining the inside of the human heart, he may ask for information on CARDIOSCOPES. A steam engineer may be concerned with the inspection of boiler tubes and a device for this purpose may have its own special name. Fourthly, the enquirer may know vaguely of the principle and for the purpose of considering the possibility of using such a device in a novel application he may request it by describing it as 'a device for seeing round corners by piping light in curved paths using the principle of total internal reflection in a bundle of fibres'. The universal retrieval system will have to provide for citation of all potentially useful designations of subjects and insofar as it does this it may fairly be said that it uses the 'objective intension' of a term or group of terms. We have above a mixture of names and a definition, but each name could, of course, be converted to its definition, which would give us a series of different definitions for the same thing, each of which would be useful for a particular subject approach.

If we are going to accept that the principle of using definitions is a desirable one, we are at once concerned with a very different kind of vocabulary, for many known names will disappear and a very sophisticated structure of basic terms becomes necessary in order to cater for all requirements without risk of inadequacy to provide for defining all potential subjects and of possible alternative ways of defining subjects, with consequent ambiguity. Moss[25] dismisses this problem as though its magnitude is of no significance, for he contends that it is solved by the principle of 'minimum vocabularies' propounded by Bertrand Russell. Russell defines a minimum vocabulary thus: 'I call a vocabulary a "minimum" one if it contains no word which is capable of a verbal definition in terms of the other words of the vocabulary.'[26] Now the principle of minimum vocabularies may well have useful application, but the statement by Moss that 'He did not wish, and no one needed, to enter into the philosophy of the argument but those who were interested would be able to find it in the work of Bertrand Russell on "minimum vocabularies" ' is dangerous stuff, for the impression is given that the compilation of minimum vocabularies is easy. Those who wish to construct a minimum vocabulary ought to read Russell for they will then be quickly disillusioned on this point. The principles on which such a vocabulary would work are made perfectly clear and so are the broad principles on which it would be constructed, but compilation in practice is a very different matter. The reader need take but the one example which Russell discusses at length, and that is the case of the incorporation of the colour 'red' in the vocabulary. He begins by considering three alternative definitions of the word 'red' which are basic 'structural' definitions manageable by minimum vocabularies and which are based on (a) position in the spectrum, (b) shade determined by range of wavelengths, and (c) the waves themselves. In spite of an exhaustive discussion of the philosophy of these alternatives, Russell finally comes to the conclusion that the word 'red' must be admitted to the vocabulary because definitions based purely on what is the concern of physics do not allow for the introduction of the idea of 'sensation', and sensation is inseparable from the concept of colour. Russell constantly warns his readers of the difficulties to be encountered in the subject of his book. He does not minimise the problems and lesser mortals than he are not going to find it easy to apply a principle whose soundness one would not presume to dispute, but whose author himself does not underestimate the difficulties.

The desirability of making provision for controlled synthesis of definitions from basic terms has been felt by workers in the information retrieval field for some time, and whilst Russell's philosophy may crystallise the matter more positively for the particular purpose he had in mind, a very similar idea can be seen to exist in the principle of 'integrative levels' which have been the subject of much discussion in the Classification Research Group in Great Britain. The positive requirement of the exclusion of terms which can be defined in other terms in the vocabulary is not consciously propounded, but the principle of building up complexes from basic simple concepts is clearly there and there is undoubtedly an analogy with the structure of a minimum vocabulary. Integrative levels are discussed by Foskett,[27] but Palmer, who quotes Foskett, doubts the utility of the principle.[28] Another example of a method of providing for the definition of terms is that of the 'vocabulary ball' of Bernier and Heumann which is mentioned above in the discussion on thesauri. It is interesting to note that practical examples of the shortcomings of a vocabulary that is not properly controlled are recorded in the documentation of the ASLIB Cranfield Research Project. Here it is reported that some failures in retrieval with the faceted classification were due to the fact that it was possible to use more than one way of indexing and a particular case is quoted in which '. . . the failure showed up the ability of the indexer or searcher to use terms which, with adjectival terms, build up expressions with the same or similar meanings'.[29] In other words the indexer had the facility of building up his own definitions from the available terminology.

The use of definitions instead of the usual names for subjects involves the splitting up of each subject into several elemental terms and these terms are found listed separately in the vocabulary. Thus, instead of using the word THERMO-METER we select from the vocabulary the words TEMPERA-TURE, MEASURING, and DEVICE. Similarly the breaking up of the ordinary name for a thing, when that name is compound, into the separate terms which comprise it involves the separate listing of these elemental terms in the vocabulary. The name THIN LAYER CHROMATOGRAPHY might be entered in a system, and searched for, by citing the three separate terms THIN, LAYERS, CHROMATOGRAPHY. (This is, of course different from a definition, which would be a very much more fundamental statement of the nature of the subject than is this accepted name.) This latter principle is very widely advocated for co-ordinate indexing systems because it can, especially with the aid of the telescoping of terms, reduce a vocabulary to a very small size, with a consequent reduction in the physical size of a file such as one comprising Uniterm or optical stencil cards. We must consider here a very important practical effect of this breaking down of subjects into elemental terms, and this is the effect which is had on the complexity of a thesaurus which attempts to provide for generic searching. It is not being argued here that provision for generic searching is necessary, but some consider that it is, and existing thesauri do attempt this provision to a greater or lesser extent.

In the classified catalogue generic survey is provided for by the very nature of the classified arrangement and in the alphabetical subject catalogue provision is made by the incorporation of 'see also' references. For co-ordinate indexing purposes a method similar to that used in the alphabetical subject catalogue is used, in that in a thesaurus instructions are given to post a given subject on to a subject which is considered to be generic to it. In a thesaurus for aeronautics, for instance, we might have:

> FOWLER FLAPS
> > Post on FLAPS
> FLAPS
> > Post on HIGH LIFT DEVICES

A search for all information on HIGH LIFT DEVICES would then pull out material on the subject in general, on particular types of such devices, e.g. FLAPS, SLATS, SLOTS, etc. and on still more specific types such as FOWLER FLAPS, SPLIT FLAPS, FIXED SLOTS, AUTOMATIC SLOTS, etc.

Now it is quite easy to build up a thesaurus which incorporates this principle and we have freedom to provide for 'posting on' to any extent we choose, providing that we are always concerned with names of things as we find them, be they simple or compound expressions. Let us see what happens, however, when we try to build up a thesaurus which provides for generic encoding, which comprises elemental terms only and not compound expressions and which telescopes words of approximately similar meanings. Suppose that in a single system we are concerned with MOVING WING TIPS which are a species of CONTROLS on aircraft, VARIABLE SPEED GEARS which are a species of TRANSMISSION SYSTEM, and END PLATES which are a species of BOUNDARY LAYER CONTROL DEVICE. Suppose also that we have telescoped terms and have suppressed MOVING in favour of VARIABLE, WINGS in favour of AEROFOILS, TIPS in favour of ENDS, SPEED in favour of VELOCITY and PLATES in favour of SHEETS, so that we have the kind of reference which says 'TIPS see ENDS', etc. We must incorporate these references in the thesaurus, together with instructions to 'post on' when a generic term is involved, and it is usual to incorporate statements which show which terms are referred from and the terms to which a given term is generic. As we are using only parts of subject designations which stand in a generic relationship one to another, the entries must be qualified in order to make the picture clear. The indexer who is entering into the system a document on MOVING WING TIPS, having been referred from TIPS by the reference 'TIPS see ENDS', must be given the instruction under ENDS: 'When used for MOVING WING TIPS, post on CONTROLS'. A similar train of instructions must follow from his turning up the other two terms in his subject, MOVING and WINGS. The final list for but three subjects and their containing heads would produce the following catastrophic result in the thesaurus:

AEROFOILS
> Standard for WINGS
> > When used for moving wing tips, post on CONTROLS

BOUNDARIES
> Generic to ENDS and SHEETS (for PLATES) as a BOUNDARY layer control device

CONTROL
> Generic to ENDS and SHEETS (for PLATES) as a boundary layer CONTROL device

CONTROLS
> Generic to VARIABLE (for MOVING), AEROFOILS (for WINGS) and ENDS (for TIPS) as CONTROLS

ENDS
> Standard for TIPS
> > When used for moving wing tips, post on CONTROLS
> > When used for end plates, post on BOUNDARIES, LAYERS and CONTROLS

GEARS
> Post on TRANSMISSION

LAYERS
> Generic to ENDS and SHEETS (for PLATES) as a boundary LAYER control device

MOVING
> See VARIABLE

PLATES
> See SHEETS

SHEETS
> Standard for PLATES
> > When used for end plates, post on BOUNDARIES, LAYERS and CONTROL

SPEED
> See VELOCITY

TIPS
> See ENDS

TRANSMISSION
>Generic to VARIABLE, VELOCITY (for SPEED) and GEARS as a TRANSMISSION system

VARIABLE
>Standard for MOVING
>>When used for moving wing tips, post on CONTROLS
>>When used for variable speed gears, post on TRANSMISSION

WINGS
>See AEROFOILS

The terms SYSTEMS in 'transmission systems' and DEVICES in 'boundary layer control devices' have not been included as they are considered to be 'unsought', i.e. not likely to be used because of their being too general. It is clear that BOUNDARIES and ENDS might have been combined, which would have made for further complication. Also we have considered only generic relations, which are but a small part of a thesaurus, for the 'related term' or 'see also' relationship is more fundamental to the structure of thesauri. It needs little imagination to see the added problems of making such references as 'MOVING WING TIPS see also AILERONS, ELEVONS', etc.

This is an exaggerated, but not unrealistic, example of what can happen if these several principles are incorporated in a thesaurus in this way. One obvious way of easing the problem is to admit the compound terms to the thesaurus for the purpose of showing what 'conventions' are used to designate them in the system, and also to give instructions regarding generic posting. The elementary terms are used in just the same way, of course and the system itself is not changed in any way. Thus an entry would appear in this form:

>MOVING WING TIPS
>>Use VARIABLE, AEROFOILS, ENDS
>>Post on CONTROLS

If generic posting is not used, then this problem does not arise, and the amount of breaking down into elemental terms, and of telescoping, can be pushed to considerable lengths. Experience will show when the resolving power of the system is beginning to suffer, but if the spread of subject matter over the field is of even distribution, the probability statistically is that a vocabulary can be reduced to quite small size. It was mentioned above that Boyd used but 427 terms. Boyd also used considerable telescoping, for in the article referred to he describes how the word HIGH is used for BIG, and LAST is used for END, so that the 'big end' of an internal combustion engine is designated in the system by the use of the words HIGH and LAST. It is significant, however, that Boyd has since announced that he now considers it unwise to break such a subject down into its several elements.[30]

The discussion of coding for information retrieval systems has been purposely omitted from this book because it is felt that it is really extraneous to the fundamental problems of subject designation. The mathematical problems of direct and superimposed coding, of the special tricks such as prime number coding, etc. are capable of solution in the contexts of particular applications. Their solution is not the solution of the basic problems of the kind discussed in this chapter and the experts in the coding field are not likely to find any difficulty in meeting our requirements when we can make quite clear what our requirements are.

REFERENCES

1 Hughes, L. E. C. (ed) *Electronic engineer's reference book*, 2nd edition, Heywood, London, 1959, p. 101.

2 Vickery, B. C. *On retrieval system theory*, Butterworths, London, 1961, pp. 45-8.

3 Morse, R. Information retrieval. *Chemical Engineering Progress*, Vol. 57, No. 5, May 1961, pp. 55-8. (Also included in A.I.Ch.E. Thesaurus, Item 9 below.)

4 Holm, B. E. Information retrieval—a solution. *Chemical Engineering Progress*, Vol. 57, No. 6, June 1961, pp. 73-8. (Also included in A.I.Ch.E. Thesaurus, Item 9 below.)

5 Patterson, H. A., Ackley, P. R. and Rehmeyer, N. B. A

system for context storage and retrieval of information from the published literature, applicable to both the IBM 101 and electronic computers. In IBM *General Information Manual*. Information retrieval systems conference, Poughkeepsie, 21st–23rd September 1959.

6   Fairthorne, R. A. An outsider inside information: USA 1961-1962. *ASLIB Proceedings*, Vol. 14, No. 11, November 1962, pp. 380-91 (p. 381).

7   Vickery, B. C. *Faceted classification: a guide to construction and use of special schemes*, Prepared for the Classification Research Group. ASLIB, London, 1960, p. 13.

8   Vickery, B. C. Thesaurus—a new word in documentation. *Journal of Documentation*, Vol. 16, No. 4, December 1960, pp. 181-9.

9   American Institute of Chemical Engineers, *Chemical engineering thesaurus: a wordbook for use with the concept co-ordination system of information storage and retrieval*. The Institute, New York, 1961.

10 Holm, B. E. and Rasmussen, L. E. Development of a technical thesaurus. *American Documentation*, Vol. 12, No. 3, July 1961, pp. 184-90.

11 Jaster, J. J., Murray, B. R. and Taube, M. *The state of the art of co-ordinate indexing*. Prepared for Office of Science Information Service, National Science Foundation. Documentation Incorporated, Washington, February 1962, p. 88.

12 Luhn, H. P. Auto-encoding of documents for information retrieval systems. In *Modern trends in documentation*, edited by M. Boaz, Pergamon Press, London, 1959, pp. 45-58.

13 ——. A statistical approach to mechanized encoding and searching of literary information. *IBM Journal of Research and Development*, Vol. 1, No. 4, October 1957, pp. 309-17.

14 Ibid., p. 314.

15 Boyd, G. M. Data retrieval from service reports. *Engineering*, Vol. 194, No. 5,036, 26th October 1962, pp. 545-8.

16   Bernier, C. L. and Heumann, K. F. Correlative indexes III. Semantic relations among semantemes—the technical thesaurus. *American Documentation*, Vol. 8, No. 3, July 1957, pp. 211-20.

17   Jaster, Murray and Taube, op. cit., pp. 99-101.

18   Jolley, J. L. Data handling by card manipulation. *Journal of Documentation*, Vol. 16, No. 3, September 1960, pp. 132-43.

19   ——. The mechanics of co-ordinate indexing and its relation to other indexing methods. Conference on co-ordinate indexing systems, London, 14th March 1963. *ASLIB Proceedings*, Vol. 15, No. 6, June 1963, pp. 161-9.

20   Shedden, D. G. Practical application of 'feature card' systems, IV. Conference on co-ordinate indexing systems, London, 14th March 1963. *ASLIB Proceedings*, Vol. 15, No. 6, June 1963, pp. 189-91.

21   Kent, A. *Textbook on mechanized information retrieval*, Interscience, New York, 1962, pp. 192-3.

22   Perry, J. W., Kent, A. and Berry, M. M. *Machine literature searching*, Interscience, New York, 1956, pp. 84-90.

23   Cohen, M. R. and Nagel, E. *An introduction to logic* (paperback edition of the first part of *An introduction to logic and scientific method*, 1934), Routledge, London, 1963, pp. 31-2.

24   Jaster, Murray and Taube, op. cit., pp. 173-5.

25   Moss, R. Discussion on morning session. Conference on co-ordinate indexing systems, London, 14th March 1963. *ASLIB Proceedings*, Vol. 15, No. 6, June 1963, pp. 160-94.

26   Russell, B. *Human knowledge: its scope and limits*, Allen and Unwin, London, 1948, pp. 94, 274-83.

27   Foskett, D. J. Classification and integrative levels. In *The Sayers memorial volume*, edited by D. J. Foskett and B. I. Palmer, The Library Association, London, 1961, pp. 136-50.

28   Palmer, B. I. *Itself an education: six lecturers on classification*, The Library Association, London, 1962, pp. 31-5.

29 Cleverdon, C. W. *ASLIB Cranfield Research Project:*
    Report on the testing and analysis of an investigation
    into the comparative efficiency of indexing systems.
    Cranfield, October 1962, p. 47.
30 Boyd, G. M. Practical application of 'feature card'
    systems, I. Conference on co-ordinate indexing systems,
    London, 14th March 1963. *ASLIB Proceedings*, Vol. 15,
    No. 6, June 1963, pp. 179-80.

7

Co-ordination and Correlation

There has long been an idea that co-ordinate indexing can do something more than any 'conventional' system can in that it is capable of showing information to exist in documents which was not known to exist at the time of indexing and could not therefore be indexed. Wyllis E. Wright, at an institute on 'The subject analysis of library materials' held at the School of Library Service, Columbia University in 1952, said 'Through a proper organisation of the various categories the researcher could discover not only what was available on a specific subject but also new combinations and comparisons of facts where relationships have never been previously recognised'.[1] J. W. Perry, at the same symposium, said 'The ability to direct searchers to new combinations not visualised at the time the documents were analysed is one of the principal advantages of machine searching methods'.[2]

Now it is not clear what Wright and Perry meant, but it would seem that they were suggesting that the co-ordination at searching of two or more terms which had been assigned to a document at indexing, but between which no relationship had been recognised by the indexer, could indicate that there was information in that document which had not previously been seen to be there. Metcalfe dismisses this idea, quite rightly, as 'utter nonsense'[3] and quotes Shaw, who referred to 'fuzzy thinking about the creation of new knowledge by assembling unrelated data mechanically'.[4, 5] Metcalfe cites as an example of this false conception the case of recorded information on the insecticide DDT, pointing out that the first record of the compound was made in 1874, there being no intimation at that time of its insecticidal properties, and that it was rediscovered and its insecticidal properties tested about

1939. At this time there was apparently one document on DDT, which did not mention insecticides, and many others on insecticides which did not mention DDT. It is obvious that no system of indexing could possibly link the information on these two quite separate subjects which appeared in separate documents which were indexed only for what they were separately about. Only the existence of the information that DDT has insecticidal powers, which would have to have appeared in at least one document, could have provided for retrieval of this information. We cannot make provision by indexing methods for the retrieval of knowledge which does not exist at the time of indexing and which cannot therefore be indexed.

Let us consider, however, a condition which might arise by chance in a retrieval system and which has relevance to this question. Suppose that we have an optical stencil card retrieval system covering records of faults in engineering components in the equipment serving an automated production line and suppose that the following sequence of events takes place. Because of loss of efficiency through an abnormally high failure rate of hydraulic seals in actuators, we decide to explore the reasons for these faults by examining the relevant records. We extract from the file the feature cards for SEALS, HYDRAULIC and ACTUATORS and stack them. We find that 247 holes are visible, which means that we have this number of records of such failures. In order to carry out our investigation methodically we decide to take a proportion of these 247 records at a time and rather than take them in, say, chronological order, we break them down by introducing another 'feature' as provided for in the retrieval system. One of the features which is recorded is the type of hydraulic fluid which is used in the actuators and five such types of fluid are provided as approved alternatives.

We decide therefore, to consider first the failure of seals when Type x hydraulic fluid was used and for this purpose we extract the feature card for Type x from the file. We expect that on stacking it with the other cards we shall reduce considerably the number of 247 relevant records already indicated, but are surprised to find that the number of our 247 holes which are occluded by the new card is only 16, leaving 231 holes still visible. The implication of this is clear: if only 16 seal failures occurred when the other four hydraulic fluids were in use and a total of 231 occurred with Type X, there must be some relationship between seal failures and the use of this type of fluid. In other words there is seen to be a correlation between a high rate of seal failures and the use of Type X hydraulic fluid.

Whilst it is not certain that Type X fluid actually causes seal failure, we have a piece of information which we didn't have before: it is likely that this type of fluid is either a direct or indirect cause of seal failure. Now we must be quite clear that this information has been generated by the system by the process of correlation and that none of the documents which comprise our records of faults contains it, for it did not exist until this moment. This is a completely different thing from the ordinary retrieval process whereby we recover existing information by the co-ordination of terms.

Because of this complete difference between the principles of co-ordination and correlation it is particularly unfortunate that the two words are now actually regarded as synonymous in the language of information retrieval and that 'correlative indexes' is just another expression for 'co-ordinate indexes'. When we speak of 'co-ordination' we mean the operations which we perform on classes in order to designate specifically what we require when we interrogate a retrieval system. This involves stating the terms which we demand must exist together (logical product), exist as alternatives (logical sum), or some of which must exist and the others of which must be absent (logical difference). If we demand from a retrieval system information on people who are six feet tall, have forty inch chests and can swim, we choose these attributes to specify the subject of our enquiry. There is no relationship between the attributes for it cannot be said that if a man is six feet tall he will have a particular size of chest or that he will or will not be a swimmer.

   The word 'correlation', however, suggests a very different
thing. It implies this very inter-dependence between things
which does not occur in the latter kind of situation. The
simplest case is that wherein the presence of one thing is an
indication of the presence (or perhaps the absence) of another.
It has been shown that if a man is a heavy cigarette smoker
he is more likely to contract lung cancer than if he does not
smoke heavily. There is said to be a 'correlation' between
cigarette smoking and the incidence of lung cancer. The
principle is fundamental to scientific work for it is often the
case that an investigation has as its specific objective the
determination of the existence or non-existence of a correlation between two or more variables. Boyle's Law is a statement of the correlation between the pressure and volume of
a gas. All other things being equal, if the pressure goes up the
volume goes down, and vice versa.
   If correlation can be found to exist between the nature of,
say, the structures of a group of chemical compounds and the
biological properties of those compounds then it is fair to say
that it may be possible to predict that a newly synthesised
compound which is known to have a structure similar to those
of the members of the group, or at least to have some
structural feature in common with them, will possess properties which are common to the group. Metcalfe did say
'All that could have been saved was the trouble of rediscover-
ing the possibility of synthesising DDT as one of a group of
organic compounds some of which were already known to
have insecticidal powers'.[4] If it was known prior to 1939 that
there was a correlation between the structure of this group
of compounds and their insecticidal properties, then it was
always possible that some chemist may by chance have noticed
that the compound dealt with in the one document which
existed was of that particular group, and so predicted that it
would have insecticidal properties. Moreover, if that document had been stored in a retrieval system so coded that it
could be retrieved by specifying its chemical structure then
because of the known correlation it might have been so
retrieved and DDT found to have the properties which it is

now known to possess. But the system could still not have been credited with having produced the information, for all that could have been searched for would have been a substance with a given structure, a structure which the substance was known at the time of indexing to possess, and by which it was therefore indexed. The fact that the substance would have been known to have insecticidal properties would have been due to prior knowledge of a 'correlation' between structure and biological activity and not to 'co-ordination' in the system, and Metcalfe's argument is still completely valid.

This is not to say, of course, that it is not possible to set up a system for the specific purpose of assisting in correlation. Computers are already used widely by statisticians for the purpose of correlating data and drawing conclusions from the fact that a given condition is usually or always found to exist whenever another set of conditions is present. The correlation between two unspecified facts may be seen to exist as a result of a statistical analysis of data, and may suggest avenues for potentially useful research. One significant condition, perhaps a feature whose cause or effect is sought may be specified, and all associated factors analysed for the purpose of trying to recognise a pattern. More positively, laboratory work may result in the formulation of a hypothesis which might be supported by the correlation of previously unrelated facts, and such correlation might demand the use of a machine such as a computer because of the mass of data to be processed. Such a machine could undoubtedly be programmed, not only to give an analysis of the data, but to present as its output only those correlations which are significant, and to this extent, given the usual requirements of adequate size of sample, etc., it could be said that such machines produce previously unknown information.

We must understand however that the kind of information which a machine is likely to be able to handle for the purpose of correlation is at present of the simplest kind only. As discussed in chapter 6 the nature of the data which may be used to describe things can be of different kinds, some being very easy to handle, some very difficult. If we consider things described by the attributes which they possess we can often set up a system which is foolproof because we can readily determine the relevant attributes and make provision for their use without risk of ambiguity or misunderstanding. The simplest form of attribute is that which can stand in isolation and which is derived by dichotomous division, e.g. 'smoker' and 'non-smoker' when used in personal histories. A little more complex is the category where a whole series of mutually exclusive terms are derived, often denoting quantity, such as the category 'age' used in medical histories. This causes no difficulty in handling. Then there is the category of the type where it is not quite so easy to make all the terms mutually exclusive. A 'colour' category may be of this kind, where the colours blue and green might be easily dealt with, but where colours which are a mixture of both might cause difficulty. We can go on isolating kinds of terms in this way until we reach terms of a completely different kind which are not attributes at all, but which name things which possess attributes (here we begin to enter the phase where we ought to consider the merits and demerits of semantic factoring, for a thing might be designated either by what it is, i.e. by its semantic factors, or by what it is called, i.e. its usual name). Still worse, there are those terms which denote human activities or subjects of study, and we reach the ultimate with terms such as 'cybernetics', 'cryogenics', etc., and the really difficult ones such as 'culture'. Straightforward correlation of the existence of simple attributes is obviously a perfectly feasible operation. When it comes to handling more complex data, however, we are up against the same problem as that which we meet in retrieval work proper, that is the fundamental one of describing things, processes, circumstances, etc., unambiguously. In certain cases there are special problems such as those of molecular structure in the chemical field, where isomerism, etc. have to be looked after.

If in the case of DDT, the necessary correlation for the prediction that the compound had insecticidal properties was merely one of showing that certain numbers of atoms of certain elements were present, or that a certain simple

F

structure formed part of the molecule, then there may have
been some justification for the claim that correlation (not
co-ordination) may have suggested the existence of these
properties. But as recently as 1958 Riemschneider promulgated
the theory that contact insecticidal activity of compounds
analogous to DDT was related to the degree of rotatability of
the molecular components.[6] The problem of coding chemical
compounds by structure is currently the subject of much
research and if this problem has not been solved, the possibility
of coding the complex features which Riemschneider considered to be significant is remote indeed! It is interesting to
note that one of Riemschneider's objects in carrying out his
work was in fact to find correlations which would enable a
compound's suitability as a pest control to be predicted. He
said: 'One series of these investigations dealt predominantly
or exclusively with fundamental principles of insecticides,
especially (1), obtaining evidence to explain the mode of
action of DDT analogues, and (2) formulating principles by
which the discovery of chemical pest control remedies now
predominantly empirical, could be placed on a systematic
basis'. Riemschneider was obviously seeking as recently as
this to find that correlation which some would have us
believe can be found by concept co-ordination methods and
machines.

Another article which illustrates the complexity of the
problem is that by Sexton on *Structure-activity relationships*.[7]
Here the word 'correlation' is used repeatedly, and its meaning
is clearly demonstrated by its context. The general problem
of predicting the biological activity of compounds by knowledge of structure and other factors is dealt with and the
techniques not merely of correlation, but of the use of hypotheses is discussed. DDT is again dealt with and different
theories regarding the effect of structure on insecticidal
properties are brought out.

The complexity of the problem as shown by these workers
in the field, is such that there seems to be little possibility of
the use of systems and machines to further this type of
research. For the simpler types of information such as that

which comprises the indication that a thing either possesses or does not possess a given attribute or that where there is possession it is possible to express the attribute quantitatively, it is obviously possible to organise systems over which there is complete control from the point of view of manipulating such data statistically and it may be possible to find associations between such attributes merely on account of the frequency of the occurrence, or perhaps non-occurrence, of two or more of them belonging to one thing. When we move away from this simple and manageable situation, we find ourselves up against problems of the designation of subjects for entry in the system which become progressively more difficult with greater complexity of the data concerned. It is this very problem which we have not solved for the purpose of retrieval systems and to think of using systems for the correlation of data for the purpose of discovering new knowledge when we are still incapable of retrieving existing knowledge satisfactorily is indeed running before we can walk. Even with the simple statistical systems, their usefulness is open to doubt for Beveridge has said that statistics are 'mainly valuable in testing an hypothesis, not in initiating a discovery. Discoveries may originate from taking into consideration the merest hints, the slightest difference in the figures between different groups, suggesting something to be followed up; whereas statistics are usually concerned with carefully prearranged experiments set up to test an idea already born'.[8] He also said 'More discoveries have arisen from intense observation of very limited material than from statistics applied to large groups. The value of the latter lies mainly in testing hypotheses arising from the former'.[9]

If it should prove possible to set up systems for the purpose of correlation with a view to discovering new knowledge, in spite of these formidable barriers, then such systems should be left to biochemists, biometricians, etc., who would use them as any other specialist uses his special apparatus. We must be quite clear about the fact that such machines are for correlating in just the same way as 'calculating' machines are for calculating and 'retrieval' machines are for retrieval. Such devices are not the business of information officers or librarians any more than are machines designed and used by other specialists, though if we can solve our own problems of subject designation we may then have a valuable contribution to make towards the problem of how such systems are to be fed. The magnitude of our own problems is seen when we consider the difficulty of the one problem of coding chemical compounds to meet the requirements of retrieving information by specifying attributes of the kind which Riemschneider's theories embrace, to say nothing of making provision for other and possibly more complex theories which have not yet appeared. Another significant question here is the effect of vocabulary controls such as role indicators, links and categorisation. The purpose of these devices is specifically to prevent retrieval of anything but the information which is designated at indexing. This is surely the very negation of the idea of searching for 'new combinations'.

In contrast to this naïve idea of being able to produce new knowledge by the mere co-ordination of terms, it is interesting to look at the work of Gray and his co-workers who did in fact investigate the possibility of retrieving information by terms other than those under which it was indexed but not, be it noted, by co-ordination, but by a kind of correlation within the system.[10] The title of the overall programme was 'Information retrieval and the design of more intelligent machines' and the general objective was the investigation of the possibility of incorporating in computers facilities which would relieve the programmer of some of his work and which would enable newer computational techniques to be better exploited because the machines would take over still more of the work which has customarily been done by human beings. As part of the programme it is stated that 'Techniques are explored for the retrieval of information having descriptors which are not the same as those under which the item was filed'.

The contrast between what is discussed here and the mistaken idea of what co-ordination can do is marked indeed, for on the one hand the philosophy is highly mathematical and abstruse, and on the other the facility aimed at is of a comparatively simple kind. That part of the work which is relevant to our subject is called by the investigators 'concept attainment'. This means the creation within the system of a satisfactory definition of the subject of search which can serve instead of that statement of the subject which the searcher uses when the latter statement has not been used in indexing the information. The reason for the need for this facility is stated thus: 'It is very likely, however, that situations will arise in which it is found that the items to be retrieved can only be described in terms of attributes that were not measured when the items were entered. This can occur either because the item classifier was not farsighted enough to appreciate the potential value of the category involved, or because it was believed that the required category could indeed be defined in terms of attributes that were measured.'

The principle is illustrated by using as an example a personnel file which contains information regarding the age, sex, education, etc., of the people concerned. Suppose that we wish to retrieve the records of all those people who are typists, but that it was not previously considered necessary to include the attribute 'typist' and that it is not possible therefore to retrieve by citing this unindexed attribute. The procedure is to create a description of typists in terms of those attributes which are used as indexing terms by the use of a sampling and correlating technique. The records for a number of people who are known to be typists are taken and the machine is required to examine these in order to find a set of attributes which are always present in the records for this category of person. In other words a set of attributes is sought such that there is a correlation between it and the attribute 'typist' so that it is then possible to say that a person with this designation is at least likely, if not certain, to be a typist.

This procedure assumes the possibility of being able in the first place to identify a sufficiently large sample of records within the system as being those for typists, with the consequent possibility of leaving it to the machine to do all that is necessary, for sufficient raw material is available to enable the machine to draw a valid conclusion. It may be, however, that it is not possible to identify many or even any records as being those for typists. In this case the machine is specially given such a record and using this as a provisional norm it retrieves other records on the basis of what it considers the appropriate description of typists to be, and each such record is checked to see whether it is or is not a record for a typist. By a process of feedback from this checking it gradually adjusts its initial description until every record it retrieves is found to be one for a typist.

The report of this work states specifically that solutions to problems such as this were sought as a means to the overall end of designing more intelligent machines, and this exercise was not carried out with the object of furthering the efficiency of retrieval systems as such. Nevertheless what is dealt with here is precisely what would be required in a retrieval system which offered the facility of retrieval by terms other than those under which information was indexed and it involves correlation as a part of the machine function. We have in fact a correlating machine within a retrieval machine, and the magnitude of the problem of correlation at this elementary level can be imagined from what is clearly shown to be involved.

Finally, the word 'correlation' has long had a very precise meaning in logic and the 'correlation of properties' is an important aspect of classification as it is dealt with in books on logic. Jevons states the principle thus: 'Things are correlated when they are so related or bound to each other that *where one is the other is, and where one is not the other is not*.'[11] Jevons goes on to give examples of such relationships including the classic case of ruminants where there is such a remarkable correlation between the various properties. In this case knowledge that a particular species of animal has cloven feet is sufficient to make it possible to predicate with certainty a great many other attributes of that species. The process suggested by Gray as described above is a method of mechanising the search for such correlation, for this will enable us to retrieve documents by using the principle that if a piece of stored information is inaccessible through the use of the name of one property it can be retrieved by citing a correlated property or properties by which the information has been indexed.

REFERENCES

1 Wright, W. E. The subject approach to knowledge: historical aspects and purposes. In *The subject analysis of library materials*, edited by M. F. Tauber, School of Library Service, Columbia University, New York, 1953, pp. 8-15 (p. 15).

2 Perry, J. W. Mechanized searching and subject headings. In *The subject analysis of library materials*, edited by M. F. Tauber, School of Library Service, Columbia University, New York, 1953, p. 200.

3 Metcalfe, J. *Subject classifying and indexing of libraries and literature*, Scarecrow Press, New York, 1959, p. 203.

4 Metcalfe, J. *Information indexing and subject cataloguing; alphabetical: classified: co-ordinate: mechanical*, Scarecrow Press, New York, 1957, p. 17.

5 Shaw, R. R. Management, machines and the bibliographic problems of the twentieth century. In *Bibliographic organization*, edited by J. H. Shera and M. E. Egan, University of Chicago Press, Chicago, 1951, pp. 200-25 (p. 201).

6 Riemschneider, R. Chemical structure and activity of DDT analogues with special consideration of their spacial structures. In *Advances in pest control research*, edited by R. L. Metcalf, Vol. 2, 1958, pp. 307-50.

7 Sexton, W. A. Structure–activity relationships. *Journal of Pharmacy and Pharmacology*, Vol. 10, 1958, pp. 465-82.

8 Beveridge, W. I. B. *The art of scientific investigation*, Heinemann, London, 1950, p. 21.

9 Ibid, p. 101.

10 Gray, H. J., Jr, and others. *Information retrieval and the design of more intelligent machines. Final report for 1st May 1958–30th June 1959 on Project ADAR, Task E.*

United States Office of Technical Services, Report PB
149 395, Washington, July 1959, pp. 136-44.
11   Jevons, W. S. *The principles of science: a treatise on logic
and scientific method.* New edition, Dover, New York,
1958, p. 681.

8

Auto-indexing and Auto-abstracting

It is generally recognised that the costliest and most difficult aspect of information storage and retrieval is the operation of input to the system. It is understandable, therefore, that considerable effort has been expended in investigating the possibility of mechanising the indexing process and the production of document summaries. Apart from this question of economics, however, there is a widespread notion that the ultimate in retrieval systems is that system which enables the whole of the content of a document to be fed into and stored in a machine. This conception is apparently based on the idea that the more of a document's content that can be recorded, the better the chance of finding that document when it is sought.

The most prolific worker in this field has been H. P. Luhn of International Business Machines Corporation. In one of his earlier papers[1] Luhn outlines his philosophy of auto-encoding on a statistical basis. He begins by discussing the process of communication between one human being and another, which he sees as the breaking down of an idea into a series of 'little ideas' and the level to which the process of breaking down extends depends on the receptivity of the addressee. The ability of the addressee to assimilate the idea is governed by the degree to which his experience of the subject field extends. The expert will need to have little breaking down of ideas, the inexperienced layman will need to have the idea explained at a most elementary level. Consequent upon this it is clear that the receptivity of the addressee will govern the number of words which must be used—the expert needs few, the layman needs many.

It seems, therefore, that if a common level of experience is a prerequisite for satisfactory communication there is also 'a common denominator for ideas between two or more individuals'. Luhn then states 'Thus the statistical probability of combinations of similar ideas being similarly interpreted must be very high'. The difficulty is that ideas are expressed in ordinary language by notions between which relationships must be expressed and because the use of language is a serial process the expression of such relationships involves the transmission of much additional information in order to build up the notions collectively into the idea which the addressor intends to convey. Data-processing machines suffer from this disadvantage for they too function on a serial basis, and the problem of providing for the exhibition of relationships is a formidable problem. Luhn suggests, therefore, that the solution is to substitute for this complex structured method of conveying ideas a purely statistical procedure based on the principle that the more elements which are common to two given statements and the more the distribution of elements in one case conforms to that in the other, the more likely it is that the two statements represent the same idea.

The practical encoding of documents is carried out by passing the whole texts of documents, in machine-readable form, through a suitable data-processing machine. Each noun which the machine encounters is converted to a standard word which represents the relevant notion, by the use of a thesaurus which is stored in the machine. If a particular notion appears with a predetermined frequency it ranks for assignment as an indexing term. This frequency can accord to particular patterns, e.g. two occurrences of a particular notion in one paragraph, and the occurrence once in one paragraph and once in either the preceding or succeeding paragraph might rank equally as qualifying conditions for assignment of the notion as an indexing term. The result of this process is a series of 'notional abstracts', one for each paragraph, which are then transferred permanently to magnetic tape reels. These reels are the records on which searching operations are performed. Searching is carried out by writing out the detailed requirements of the searcher, in essay form, processing this essay in the machine by exactly the same technique as is used for entering documents into the system, and finally looking for a match between its notional abstracts and those in the store. Complete matches are not expected, of course, but a certain minimum percentage match is specified. It is also suggested that searches might subsequently be refined in the light of the results of the initial run of the machine.

In an article published a little later than that discussed above, Luhn describes a method for the automatic production of literature abstracts.[2] The principles used here are basically the same as those propounded in the first paper, but they are extended to serve the specific purpose of abstracting and the use of a thesaurus does not enter into the process. The idea of the determination of word significance on the basis of frequency of occurrence and relative positions of the several occurrences of a given significant word is preserved, but the concentration of different significant words at any point is also measured. This concentration is stated as a 'significance factor' which is determined in the following way. Once significant words have been identified, their distance from each other is measured in terms of the number of non-significant words occurring between any pair. If a pair is separated by no more than a predetermined number of non-significant words (Luhn states that an analysis of documents has shown that this figure should be four or five) then the relationship is significant. Clusters of words will be found which are comprised of several different significant words and significant relationships and the significance factor is determined by dividing the square of the number of significant words by the total number of words in the cluster. Thus if we had a statement such as: 'BLOWN FLAPS on SWEPTBACK WINGS of this ASPECT RATIO caused INSTABILITY at FLARE-OUT', and the words in capitals had been determined as significant, we should have eight significant words and a total of thirteen words. The significance factor would then be the square of 8 divided by 13 which equals 4.9. (The process in practice is a little more complex than this, but this is the basic principle.) The significance factors for the clusters are now arranged in descending order of magnitude by the machine and the sentence containing that cluster with the highest ranking, or more likely the first two, three, or four sentences in the list are printed out as they stand to form the 'auto-abstract'.

The philosophy on which Luhn bases this theory is summed up thus: '. . . whatever the topic, the closer certain words are associated, the more specifically an aspect of the subject is being treated. Therefore, wherever the greatest number of frequently occurring different words are found in greatest physical proximity to each other, the probability is very high that the information being conveyed is most representative of the article.' It need hardly be pointed out that this is not the way in which a human abstractor does his work, nor is an auto-abstract the same kind of thing as that produced by a human being. Fairthorne makes the telling point that this procedure is more properly regarded as 'auto-quotation' than 'auto-abstracting'.[3]

In another and slightly later article Luhn describes a further refinement for the purpose of auto-encoding.[4] Whereas the principle formerly described produced groups of terms derived from a thesaurus, each group being determined by the occurrence of its constituent terms within a paragraph, but without any regard to the particular relationships between the terms, it is here suggested that account ought to be taken of such relationships. A method is described of recording the fact that two significant terms are found in immediate proximity to each other (discounting the existence of common words such as articles, conjunctions, prepositions, etc.) and marshalling such word pairs to form the indexing terms. Two groups of significant terms are taken, the first being those of highest significance rating (say the first sixteen words), and the second being a group of the following words down to a suitable significance rating. The first group terms are referred to as 'nodes' and for this reason the resulting index is referred to as a 'nodal index'. Proximity between a pair of first order words is regarded as a significant relationship and so is that between a first order word and a second order word. Any first order word is likely, of course, to be so related to several other words and the resulting list which the machine produces is a list of first order words (nodes) with each showing the several different words to which it has been found in the text to be related. Luhn shows an example of the auto-encoding of a medical article and typical resulting index entries are:

ATTACK   Cholesterol, Heart
BLOOD   Level, Lowering, Develop, Cholesterol

The complete list of such entries is stored, in code, on punched cards, punched tape, or magnetic tape and this forms the record to be searched in the retrieval process.

These pioneering efforts do not seem to have been developed further by Luhn himself or by other workers. A more general article which appeared two years later indicated that Luhn still advocated the principles which he had at first propounded.[5] Another worker at IBM, however, reported only slightly later than the early work of Luhn a rather different approach to automatic indexing. Phyllis Baxendale investigated the effectiveness of the machine-selection of indexing terms by three different methods and tabulated the results for comparison.[6] The first method simply selected nouns and adjectives on the criterion of frequency of occurrence, after having deleted non-significant words such as articles, conjunctions, etc. by reference to a prepared list of such unwanted terms. The second method selected nouns and adjectives from 'topic sentences' only. Topic sentences were those which appeared as the first and last sentences in paragraphs for it had been found by analysis that it was these whose information content was most significant. The third method was to select phrases from the text, because it was argued that phrases, which comprise combinations of nouns and modifiers together with a preposition, are the most useful parts of the text as far as indication of subject content is concerned. The selection process was based on the location of prepositions, and the words in the phrases so located were extracted to serve as indexing terms. The amount by which each of these three methods reduced the size of the original text is of interest. The greatest condensation was achieved by the prepositional phrase method and this was also considered to be the most successful in selecting suitable indexing terms.

Rath, Resnick and Savage, also of IBM have carried out investigations which used Luhn's methods of selecting significant parts of text, and one of these assessed the relative effectiveness of using as guides to the subject content of documents: (a) the titles only of the documents, (b) auto-abstracts, (c) pseudo-auto-abstracts, and (d) the full texts of the documents.[7] A pseudo-auto-abstract is formed by using the same number of sentences extracted from a document as would be used for a Luhn-type auto-abstract (ten per cent of the total) but the sentences are simply those which comprise the first five per cent and the last five per cent of the article. The test was carried out by providing different groups of people with these different sources and, with a time limit of course, finding which kind of source best enabled the people to assess the relevance of the documents to carefully selected questions. It was found that in assessing the relevance of documents by the four methods, the success of the people tested was directly related to the actual percentage of the answers which were contained in the four types of source material. The full texts, of course, contained all the answers, the auto-abstracts contained twenty-five per cent, the pseudo-auto-abstracts eighteen per cent and the titles only one per cent. (This latter figure is a significant pointer to the maximum possible effectiveness of KWIC indexing based on titles!)

In another investigation these three workers compared the standards of sentence selection achieved by five different criteria in auto-abstracting.[8] They also investigated the variation in such selection between six human selectors, and finally compared the work of the machines with that of the humans. The machine abstracting was again basically Luhn-type and the only difference between the five methods was in the formulas used to calculate significance factors of the 'clusters'. Two of the conclusions reached were that there was little variation between the several machine methods, and that there was considerably more variation between the several human indexers. The extraordinary thing about this is the implication that there is some significance in these results. It can hardly be expected that there will be much difference in results from operations which are based on the same fundamental criteria, with but slight (and apparently arbitrarily assigned) differences in modification. Much worse than this, of course, is the premise, which may prove to be quite false, that the sentences which the machines selected so consistently are the best for the purpose. Much the most important conclusion was that, in the words of the investigators themselves, 'There was very little agreement between the subjects and machine methods in their selection of representative sentences.' The word 'subjects', of course, refers to the human selectors. Further investigation of the selection of sentences is reported by Resnick and results of the measurement of consistency are given.[9]

Before leaving the subject of machine indexing on Luhn's principles, and the work which has been done at IBM subsequent to Luhn's original work, it is interesting to note the line of investigation which Baxendale has taken in more recent times. In a paper presented at the Third Institute on Information Storage and Retrieval held 13th–17th February 1961, she outlined a study of the principles on which indexing terms should be selected from titles of documents.[10] The approach was quite sophisticated and may have been sound, but the significant thing is that work on titles is a far cry from the ambitious project of digesting entire texts, which ground the pioneering work of Luhn first broke. From current reports it appears that Baxendale is still working at the title and paragraph caption level, though work is also being carried out at IBM, Yorktown Heights, New York, under Kochen, which involves 'experimentation with three techniques for clustering and ranking similar sentences or words in a text, based on co-occurrence statistics'.[11]

There have, of course, been investigations of variations of Luhn's basic theories, and an interesting one is that carried out by Edmundson and his co-workers.[12, 13] These investigators borrowed a principle from information theory which suggested that the significance of a word should be a function of rarity, rather than frequency of appearance, but it should be made quite clear that rarity was to mean the infrequency of appearance of a word in general usage, not in a given document. The frequency of appearance of a word within a document was then taken in conjunction with this measure of rarity to give the significance factor of the word, and it was suggested that either $f-r$ or f/r would be a suitable expression for significance, where f was the frequency of occurrence in the document and r the frequency in general usage. Thus a word used rarely for ordinary purposes which appeared frequently in a document would have its significance rating for that document very much amplified whilst normally rare words used rarely and common words used frequently would all receive low ratings. It was contended that this principle of 'relative frequency' would give greater discrimination than Luhn's method in that it would distinguish between common and rare words used with equal frequency within a document, a thing which Luhn's method did not do, and would also eliminate general words normally rejected by the use of 'stop lists'. This work, which is reported more fully in an article by Edmundson and Wyllys,[14] seems to have been entirely theoretical and no practical work is mentioned.

Another investigation of the signifiance of word frequency has been made at the Computation Laboratory, Harvard University. Storm describes experiments to test the hypothesis 'that those parts of a text for which the number of initial occurrences of nouns is greater than average for the document are likely to be of special interest for the determination of document content'.[15] The approach here seems to be a mixture of abstruse mathematics and trial and error, but the author treats the subject quite dispassionately, makes no extravagant claims and makes it clear that this may be but one of several factors to be taken into account in identifying significant areas of text. Having tabulated the appearance of 'first nouns' throughout a text, a graph is drawn of their incidence, and the peaks are expected to show the relevant significant areas.

Various techniques such as moving averages and weighting are applied to the graph in order to re-shape it to conform more satisfactorily to what it is considered the analysis should have produced, and consideration is given to progressive modification of the criteria as the scanning proceeds through the text, to allow for the fact that first appearances are likely to be fewer towards the end than they are at the beginning. Two quite difficult mathematical papers were used as texts for the purpose of the investigation and the style of the second was more discursive than the first. Because of this difference in style, the method was found to be less successful with the second paper than with the first, and the results in general were stated to be inconclusive.

The foregoing has dealt exclusively with the processing of text for the purpose of extracting from it those parts which serve either or both of the two problems of automatic indexing and automatic abstracting. As far as indexing is concerned, this procedure is the automation of the *input* to a retrieval system. There is, of course, an alternative to this, and that is to store the whole of a text in the system and to automate searching by providing for machine matching of requests with the stored text. This approach has been developed at Thompson Ramo Wooldridge Inc, where the philosophy of Swanson has been that if a computer technique for retrieval from full text cannot be developed it is out of the question to consider the use of a computer to operate on an abbreviated form of the text such as an index.[16] Successful processing of full text is therefore a prerequisite to development of automatic indexing techniques and such full-text processing has been the subject of the work at the Ramo-Wooldridge Laboratories.

The results of this work are reported in *Current research* by H. P. Edmundson *et al.*[17] With the full texts of the documents in the collection stored in machine-readable form, a search request is formulated by taking the question in natural-language form and feeding it to the machine, which looks up the words of the question in a thesaurus and converts the wording to a form likely to provide maximum chance of successful matching. The processed question is then run against the whole store of texts and the output consists of a list of document numbers ordered according to the machine's assessment of relevance rating. The results are considered to be indicative of the feasibility of automatic indexing of acceptably high quality at economic cost. One very interesting aspect of this work is that it was found that allowing the machine to formulate its own question from the original natural language question resulted in greater success in retrieval than was the case when the question was prepared for input to the machine by a human being. The conclusion is drawn that 'This result came about simply because it is more important for retrieval purposes to be thorough (with the formulation of synonyms and near-synonyms) than it is to be clever.'

Looking at the overall picture of automatic indexing and automatic abstracting, there seem to be two important questions which impinge on the prospect of success. The first one is whether the techniques which are likely to be available are capable of summarising document content in such a way that the summaries are truly representative of the overall content of a document. The methods used so far seem to suffer from the defect that though they pick out significant parts of text these parts are not sufficient in themselves, either separately or in combination, to give the sort of picture which a human abstractor or indexer would provide by viewing the whole of the text and digesting it as such, rather than by lopping off whole chunks in order to leave a residue of the author's own words. Hence Fairthorne's distinction between 'auto-abstracting' and 'auto-quotation'. Matching of such isolated pieces of information may not provide a satisfactory retrieval basis and it is not even safe to assume that such matching can be done with any degree of sophistication in the first place, for practical work has shown that such word groups must be very restricted to ensure satisfactory recall. Ray observed that 'It's clear that the average score on element retrieval could have been substantially improved by cautioning the members of the requesting panel to use phrases of length three or more words only with extreme care.'[18] This seems highly restrictive. Fairthorne has also warned of the danger of assuming that it is possible to match natural language satisfactorily: '. . . only by rare chance were ordinary verbal statements so directly associated with sets of documents that a conjunction of such statements corresponded with the intersection of the sets.'[19]

The methods used to date for the selection of words and sentences for the purposes of the provision of indexing terms and the compilation of abstracts are inordinately crude in spite of the very clever tricks which have been performed with computers. It is a very big step from these very creditable attempts to methods which simulate human processing of texts, because of the concentration of machines on comparatively isolated portions of text, once such areas have been identified, as distinct from the complex processes of assimilation and subsequent summary by a human mind. A very interesting step has been taken in this direction, however, by the work of Doyle, for the result of the operations on text by his methods is to provide a more coherent picture of the whole than seems to be possible with other methods.

In an article aptly entitled *Semantic road maps for literature searchers* Doyle describes a process for computer analysis of text which first produces association lists of significant terms in a document, but the methods used are of a more sophisticated nature than those described earlier.[20] Much has been made in other methods of the significance of adjacency of words to each other, and whilst Doyle takes this into account, one of the direct results of his method is to combine word pairs once and for all, i.e. to produce compound terms, if frequency of adjacent pairing in the text justifies it. Other significant occurrences of the presence of pairs of words, regardless of proximity, is taken into account however and this seems to be one feature which frees selection from the disadvantage of concentration on localised groups of significant words. Doyle makes a clear distinction between mere proximity and what he considers to be the semantic import of co-occurrence regardless of distance between the words concerned. The former i.e. the occurrence of words next to each other he calls 'language redundancy' and the latter, i.e. significant co-occurrence regardless of proximity he calls 'reality redundancy'.

This procedure produces lists of words and against each word there appears a list of those words with which it is associated, and the number of documents in which each association of a pair of terms has appeared. This complex structure of associations is then displayed as a two-dimensional diagram which indicates the strengths of the various associations by quoting this occurrence-rating between pairs. Doyle is anticipating the availability of equipment which will perform this complex operation automatically, and he admits to this, but he foresees the display of these 'semantic road maps' on a TV-like screen, and the appropriate network for beginning a search is selected by citing a keyword. The map displayed as a result of this is in effect a 'small scale' map in that a great many associations are shown. The searcher is guided by this picture to select one or more other promising terms, the choice of which he indicates by typing out the selected word on a typewriter-like keyboard, or perhaps, as described in a later article,[21] pointing to the word on the screen with a 'light gun'. This selection calls up a 'larger scale' map which shows these two expressions and their more detailed associations, and further narrowing down of the field can be achieved by further word selection until one or but a few documents have been selected on the basis of whole patterns of word associations. This is an example, of course, of a useful application of the word-association lists discussed in chapter 6 and Doyle is working on the assumption that the principle, also discussed there, of using machines to suggest to searchers what they ought to be looking for, is a valid one. In support of this assumption he quotes the work of Maron who predicted, and Stiles who confirmed by experiment, that retrieval accuracy is increased by the use of associations.

This view is shared, of course, by the contemporary protagonists of classificatory methods such as Vickery, who says 'An information retrieval system, if it is to help the user to find his way about the mass of information relating to a certain field of knowledge, must therefore be designed (1) to help even the ignorant user to pass from the vague formulation of a subject in his mind to its precise formulation in the system, and (2) having reached this precise formulation, to direct him forward to literature references relating to it'[22] and '. . . classification is essential in all forms of subject indexing, in order to reveal the pattern of knowledge to the searcher.'[23] Foskett has been quick to invoke Doyle to support the idea that classification is necessary to exploit the principle of association and quotes him as saying 'hierarchies have been, and still are important. They provide familiar conceptual grooves by which people can steer themselves to areas of interest'.[24] Whether there is so much common ground between the classificationists and the machine-men is open to doubt. It does seem likely that systems such as Doyle's will be a better guide to relevance of documents than those systems which produce indexing terms in comparative isolation, for a more general picture of overall subject content is presented to the searcher. Moreover, we seem to have here the first signs of the re-introduction of 'browsability' which was lost virtually completely when machines were first brought into use.

As classification has been mentioned, it might be appropriate to consider here work which has been directed at what is regarded by the investigators as automatic 'classification' rather than automatic indexing. Maron reports an experiment designed to explore the possibility of automatically assigning texts to predetermined categories by assessing relevance to the respective categories on the basis of word association.[25] A group of 260 'documents' was taken as the raw material for determining the relations between 'clue words' found in documents and the categories comprising the classification. The documents were in fact abstracts taken from IRE *Transactions on electronic computers* and the thirty-two categories used were specially devised to suit the subject field under consideration.

The first step was the careful assignment to one or more categories of each document, by a human indexer. The whole text of each document was then processed by machine for the purpose of analysis of the word content of the entire collection and by a series of steps of elimination, including the rejection of non-significant words such as articles and prepositions, of significant but infrequently occurring words, etc., a residue of about a thousand different words was reached. Each of these thousand words was then examined in relation to the documents contained in the first category, then in relation to those in the second category, etc. Clearly, where the number of occurrences of a given word was significantly higher in those documents belonging to one category than in those belonging to other categories that word could be considered to be a useful clue word. Thus the list of a thousand words was whittled down to a final ninety clue words by eliminating those which showed no such significance.

By applying the calculus of probability a formula was now developed which enabled the machine to predict the subject category to which a document belonged by reading and analysing the text. This formula took into account such factors as the ratio between the number of entries which had occurred in a given category (i.e. the number of documents assigned to it) and the total number of entries made for the entire collection, the ratio between the number of occurrences of a given word in the documents in a given category and the total number of occurrences of all clue words in all documents in that category. The purpose of this part of the experiment was to provide these values by working on the selected 260 documents, and the characteristics of these documents therefore determined what the values should be. Assuming that the documents were reasonably representative it was fair to assume that the criteria derived empirically in this way would serve for the indexing of all documents in the subject field. The same documents were in fact classified by the machine after the method had been developed, and a second set of entirely new documents, 145 in number, was used to test the effectiveness of the method.

The experiment was moderately successful and it was concluded that the probability that the category selected by the machine for a given document was the correct one was 84·6 per cent. This was for the overall picture, but the figure was down to 48·7 per cent in cases where the number of clue words in a document was down to one. The figures for the second set of documents (whose characteristics had not been allowed to affect the indexing criteria in any way) were, not surprisingly, considerably poorer. To take an actual comparison, the probability of success in the first group when documents had been assigned to just one category and the number of different clue words in each document was at least two, was 91·1 per cent. The figure for the same set of conditions in the second group was only 50 per cent.

An attempt to refine Maron's method of automatic classification was made by Borko and Bernick.[26] The same groups of documents as those used by Maron were taken as the basis of the experiment in order to compare the results with Maron's findings, and the latter's ninety clue words were also adopted. There were two important differences in the processes used, however. The first of these was that the compilation of the classification, i.e. the derivation of the categories, was based on machine analysis of the texts, whereas Maron's categories were determined entirely by humans. This was accomplished by building a matrix of word associations from the data provided by the machine and, using a technique known as 'factor analysis', producing a number of 'factors' comprising groups of words with computed loadings, each of these factors forming the raw material for a category. The number of factors so produced was twenty-one and each was examined by the investigators and converted to a category by giving it an appropriate name. The philosophy behind this procedure, which seems to be an eminently sensible one, was that if the same data as that to be used for automatic classification of documents were used for creating the classification then a classification of maximum hospitality would be produced.

The second difference was in the actual technique used for assigning the documents to categories in the process of automatic classification. Each category had related to it a number of the ninety clue words which had been found to be significant as far as that category was concerned. Each such term

was given a 'factor loading' which was a measure of its usefulness in predicting membership of that category by a document which contained it. A document was then classified by
counting the number of times such a significant word
appeared and, for each category to which the word belonged,
multiplying the appropriate factor loading of the word by
the number of occurrences. If more than one significant word
belonging to a single category appeared in a document, the
results for all such multiplications were summed. The document was then assigned to the category with the highest score.

The results of indexing the first group of documents compared poorly with those of Maron, but the second group was
handled with almost the same efficiency as that provided
by Maron's method. The results on the second group, are of
course the more significant because these documents had
played no part in providing data on which the procedures
were based. Nevertheless Borko and Bernick's results were
rather disappointing and they suggest that the explanation
is that they erroneously mixed two quite separate subjects of
experiment (a) the construction of the classification and (b)
the technique of automatic classification.

Maron regards the words 'classifying' and 'indexing' as
synonymous and uses them interchangeably in the abstract
at the head of his paper. Borko and Bernick actually entitled
their report 'Automatic document classification'. What all
these investigators actually worked on were, of course, classification schemes of the most elementary kind, and the results
of automatic classification by such schemes are little different
from the assigning of subject headings, or indexing terms to
documents. The important thing about methods such as this
is the nature of the headings assigned to documents. It was
suggested above that the advantage of Doyle's methods is that
a broader picture of a document's subject content is provided
than is possible with the selection of isolated terms or groups
of terms from the document. It seems reasonable to suppose
that the names of subject categories are also likely to serve
better as indicators of subject content on the same grounds,
for in the nature of things they contain a document's subject,

which is a very different thing from the capability of isolated index words which may be only a part of what is required to provide an adequate description of a subject. The trouble is, of course, that the classification discussed in these articles is so coarse as to be analogous to that used in publications such as *Chemical Abstracts* where classification is useful for current awareness but is of limited use for retrospective search. The very much more specific subject indexes are resorted to for this purpose. This is not to suggest that refinement would not facilitate 'classification' under much more specific headings.

It seems that the work reviewed above can be divided into four principal kinds:

(a) That which uses the principle of selection of individual words on the basis of frequency counts and assessment of relative position, with the production of an index for consultation by machine (e.g. Luhn).

(b) That which provides for scanning of full texts at the time of search, without any prior processing of the texts (e.g. Swanson, Edmundson).

(c) That which produces displays of two-dimensional word patterns of a text at various levels of specificity to enable the searcher to work his way through the store systematically (Doyle).

(d) That which classifies documents by assigning them to predetermined categories, thus providing a classified listing for human consultation (Maron, Borko and Bernick).

There is one feature which all these methods have in common, and this is the avoidance of any attempt to reckon with the problem of semantics, that is with the meaning of the texts which are processed. All the data which are used are of a purely statistical nature. If the methods have any success, then this stems from the principle that if a statistical similarity is found to exist between two texts then there is likely to be a similarity of meaning. The important thing is that it is possible to establish that a similarity of meaning exists without

being concerned in the slightest degree with what that meaning is. The ingenious feature of the methods discussed here
is that they all exploit this idea by assigning to machines
what machines can do well, i.e. the counting and sorting of
vast quantities of things, whilst retaining for human handling
only a minimum of intellectual activity in the form of the
semantic problem of expressing a search requirement. Communication begins, of course, with the creation of a document
and the author is clearly concerned with semantics in that he
must inject into the document the meaning of what he intends
to convey. There is, however, no need to be concerned further
with semantics until the searcher specifies his requirements
(a) in the form of a written statement to be processed by the
machine and then compared with the indexing data for a
Luhn-type system, (b) in the form of a written statement to
be processed by the machine and then compared with the full
texts in the store for an Edmundson-type system, (c) in the
form of a single keyword for the calling up of a 'semantic
road map' for a Doyle-type system, and (d) in the form of a
class or category name for a Maron-type system.

It is often intimated that problems of machine translation
have a great deal in common with those of automatic abstracting and indexing, but it seems that the work done on machine
translation has been aimed, understandably, at syntactic
analysis and as syntax is inextricably bound up with meaning, this can only be construed as an attempt to facilitate
the conversion of one language to another by taking meaning
into account in the intermediate stage. Some writers imply
that syntactic analysis is potentially useful in the field of
information retrieval and Garvin argues that greater accuracy and reliability should ensue from the use of a system
which reduces texts and search requests to the system
language on the basis of semantic criteria.[27]

It is not surprising that views have been expressed regarding the relative difficulty of machine indexing and machine
translation. Garvin considers that information retrieval problems are more severe than those of machine translation because whereas in the latter '. . . the major objective is one

of recognising the content of a document in order to render it in a different language' automatic indexing and automatic abstracting require further processing of the content for 'Content processing thus involves not only the recognition but also the evaluation of content, since for both indexing and abstracting pertinent relevance judgements have to be applied'. At the same conference as that at which Garvin made the above comments, Bohnert said 'The machine input problem for auto-abstracting is even more serious than for machine indexing. Abstracts must preserve the message of the original document while indexing merely needs to indicate the subject matter of a document. Mechanical translation also suffers severely from the machine input problem.[28] One can only assume from this, on the grounds that mechanical translation must 'preserve the message of the original document' that Bohnert considered that machine translation is more difficult than machine indexing, which view is opposed to that of Garvin.

Which of these views proves to be correct will depend on what processes are eventually found to be necessary in the two respective fields, assuming that both automatic indexing and machine translation prove to be practicable. At the present time Bohnert's view seems likely to prevail, but not for the reason which she advances. Automatic indexing is being investigated mainly on the lines of statistical analysis and this seems to be very much easier than the process of syntactic analysis with which machine translation is necessarily encumbered. Machine translation, it seems, must always involve the formalisation of language and this has proved to be a formidable task. Indeed it may prove to be impossible, and the view is often expressed that this will surely prove to be the case. Mortimer Taube, in a scathing attack on machine translation, contends that the lack of success of efforts which have been made continuously since 1946 is evidence of the futility of trying to solve the problem.[29]

If it is assumed that statistical analysis proves in the long run to be inadequate for automatic indexing and abstracting, and that semantic criteria must be used, then the problems of information retrieval are placed on the same footing as machine translation and the comparative difficulty of achieving success in the several fields needs to be reconsidered. It seems likely that Garvin's contention that automatic indexing will be the more difficult will prove to be right, for the reasons which he gives.

This brings us to the second important question which is likely to affect the problem of automation. There has been an assumption in the work done to date on automatic indexing and automatic abstracting which may be perfectly valid but which, if it proves to be false, may alter very considerably the degree of difficulty of achieving acceptable quality in indexes and abstracts. This is the assumption that what a document says is the same thing as the subject about which it says what it has to say. Bohnert's reference to the 'message' and the 'subject matter' of a document in the statement quoted above is too casual to suggest that she was trying to make the distinction which is being attempted here, but the concept of the 'message' and the 'subject' of a document being two different things goes to the heart of the matter, for what a document says can be regarded as its message and what it is about as its subject.

Let us take an example of manageable proportions and try to distinguish between the two concepts. In *Journal of Applied Physics* for April 1960 there appeared a letter entitled 'Method for determining the thermal conductivity of incandescent solids'.[30] The abstract of this letter which appeared in *Physics Abstracts* read as follows: 'The paper gives an analysis and brief description of a method using a cylindrical sample heated at one end and whose temperature is measured at three points: (1) the heated end, (2) the middle and (3) the top surface. Results are given for (*a*) graphite and (*b*) uranium dioxide. Agreement with published values is obtained for (*a*) but not for (*b*), indicating the need for further investigation.' The title of this letter is a statement of the subject of the document, and a very good one at that, but it is clear that what the document says, which is summarised in the abstract, is the author's 'message' about that subject and it would be futile to try to match these two statements by any machine method advanced so far. It would be quite wrong to leave the impression here that the letter itself yields no more useful indexing data than this very brief abstract does, but the nature of the abstract has been used as an indication of the nature of the text of a document as distinct from the subject of the text. In the letter the expression 'thermal conductivity' appears repeatedly, so do the words 'temperature' and 'emissivity', but the word 'incandescent' does not appear once, and 'solids' is used only in the opening sentence, which is almost a repeat of the title. The point is that sometimes at least it is the case that an author states the subject of his article in the title and thereafter finds it unnecessary to repeat the words used there as his intention has been made clear once and for all. As in the case cited above, he may find it necessary to repeat some of them but not others and this is sufficient to eliminate the possibility of satisfactory indexing on the basis of word frequency counts. The incorporation in an index of the expression 'thermal conductivity' is obviously a necessary and useful step which a machine would take in this case, but the coarseness of the indexing without further qualification, because of the absence of other words such as 'incandescent', is likely to be unacceptable.

It is not suggested, of course, that indexing should be done from titles, but that titles do typify statements of subjects. In a document which gives an account of a piece of scientific or technical work there may be, and often are, subsidiary subjects which may justify special treatment by the indexer, because of their being units of information in their own right and which, for that reason, may be useful outside the context of the document, but which the title is unlikely to mention. Details of the construction of a special instrument may have value in another application, the effects of a chemical, or a process, on the properties of a material may be observed and recorded, though they are incidental to the work in hand, and such information obviously justifies provision being made for its recovery. Each and every unit of information in a document, including its overall subject, should be treated as

though it comprised the subject of a separate document and
entry in the system provided accordingly. It is the desirability
of providing this sort of treatment for documents which leads
to the idea of recording the entire contents of documents by
feeding them into the system, but the important thing is to
isolate the individual units of information, treat them as
though they comprised separate documents, and provide subject designations which will match an inquirer's statement
of requirements to which a unit may be relevant.

It is easy to be tempted to think that the wonderful achieve-
ments resulting from the application of computers to all sorts
of problems are a pointer to their capabilities in the field of
information retrieval. The most relevant cases are naturally
considered to be those which operate on the same kind of
material as that with which information retrieval is concerned, i.e. textual material. The success of the work of fill-
ing in the gaps in the Dead Sea Scrolls is well known. Lesser
known work such as the analysis of the 'Quintus Curtius
Snodgrass' letters which showed fairly conclusively that they
were not written by Mark Twain did not even require the use
of a machine, and a statistical analysis which enabled word
frequency to be plotted against word length was all that was
required to provide very consistent and convincing evidence.[31] In cases of this sort where the probability of what a
missing word is, or where establishment of authorship, are
concerned, it is merely the form of the texts which is relevant and similarity of form is apparently not difficult to
recognise. Similarity of meaning in two texts is also likely
to be recognisable, without knowing what the meaning is,
and workers such as Luhn and Edmundson have provided
evidence, though this may not be conclusive, which supports
this theory. This problem is likely to be more difficult, however, than recognising similarity of form. One step more
difficult still seems to be the problem of machine translation,
where the message of a text must have its meaning extracted
and then re-structured in a new language, but we are at least
still concerned with 'message' only. Perhaps yet more difficult
is the formulation of auto-abstracts (not auto-quotations),

because the message has to be digested and it is not merely a case of re-casting an entire message in another form as with machine translation.

Finally we reach what may prove to be the most difficult of all processes—automatic indexing. The reason for this contention is that, on the basis of the argument advanced above, there is a difference between the subject and the message of a document. We are no longer concerned with re-casting or even reducing a text, but with the conversion of message to subject, or in other words determining from what a document says what that document is about. What a document says is what a searcher hopes to learn about the subject after successful retrieval and clearly he cannot feed what a document says to a machine for matching purposes for he does not know this until retrieval is accomplished. What a document says is of interest to us at the output stage, when it may tell us, and must, if it is to be of use to us at all, something which we didn't know before and which, because we didn't know it before, we could not have fed into the machine in the first place in order to ask the machine to find a document containing it. If we are limited to matching what is already known to exist in the literature because of these methods of automatic indexing, then it is surely the case that the simple law will apply that the probability of recovering a document will vary inversely with the novelty of what it has to say. Novelty is surely the essence of progress, and progress is not going to be served by a system which has an enormous capacity but which stultifies the exploitation of new discoveries.

REFERENCES

1   Luhn, H. P. A statistical approach to mechanised encoding and searching of literary information. *IBM Journal of Research and Development*, Vol. 1, No. 4, October 1957, pp. 309-17.
2   ———. The automatic creation of literature abstracts. *IBM Journal of Research and Development*, Vol. 2, No. 2, April 1958, pp. 159-65.

3   Fairthorne, R. A. An outsider inside information: USA 1961–1962. *ASLIB Proceedings*, Vol. 14, No. 11, November 1962, pp. 380-91 (p. 386).

4   Luhn, H. P. Auto-encoding of documents for information retrieval systems. In *Modern trends in documentation*, edited by M. Boaz, Pergamon Press, London, 1959, pp. 45-58.

5   ——. Automated intelligence systems—some basic problems and prerequisites for their solution. In *The Clarification, unification and integration of information storage and retrieval. Proceedings of February 23rd, 1961 Symposium*, edited by E. A. Tomeshi and others, Special Libraries Association, New York, 1961, pp. 3-20.

6   Baxendale, P. B. Machine-made index for technical literature—an experiment. *IBM Journal of Research and Development*, Vol. 2, No. 4, October 1958, pp. 354-61.

7   Rath, G. J., Resnick, A. and Savage, T. R. Comparisons of four types of lexical indicators of content. *American Documentation*, Vol. 12, No. 2, April 1961, pp. 126-30.

8   ——. The formation of abstracts by the selection of sentences. Part I: Sentence selection by men and machines. *American Documentation*, Vol. 12, No. 2, April 1961, pp. 139-41.

9   Resnick, A. The formation of abstracts by the selection of sentences. Part II: The reliability of people in selecting sentences. *American Documentation*, Vol. 12, No. 2, April 1961, pp. 141-3.

10 Baxendale, P. B. An empirical model for machine indexing. In The American University, Center for Technology and Administration, *Machine indexing: progress and problems. Papers presented at the Third Institute on Information Storage and Retrieval, February 13–17th 1961*, pp. 207-18.

11 National Science Foundation, *Current research and development in scientific documentation*, No. 11, November 1962, pp. 111-18.

12 ibid., No. 5, October 1959, pp. 33-4.

13 ibid., No. 6, May 1960, pp. 43-4.

14 Edmundson, H. P. and Wyllys, R. E. Automatic abstracting and recommendations. *Communications of the ACM*, Vol. 4, No. 5, May 1961, pp. 226-34.

15 Storm, E. Some experimental procedures for the identification of information content. In Harvard University, Computation Laboratory, Scientific Report No. ISR-1, *Information storage and retrieval*, 30th November 1961, pp. I-1 to I-34.

16 Swanson, D. R. Searching natural language text by computer. *Science*, Vol. 132, No. 3434, 21st October 1960, pp. 1099-104.

17 National Science Foundation, op. cit., No. 11, November 1962, pp. 155-7.

18 Ray, L. C. Automatic indexing and abstracting of natural languages. In *The clarification, unification and integration of information storage and retrieval. Proceedings of February 23rd, 1961 Symposium*, edited by E. A. Tomeshi and others, Special Libraries Association, New York, 1961, pp. 85-94.

19 Fairthorne, R. A. Discussion on afternoon session. Conference on co-ordinate indexing systems, London, 14th March, 1963. *ASLIB Proceedings*, Vol. 15, No. 6, June 1963, pp. 160-94.

20 Doyle, L. B. Semantic road maps for literature searchers. *Journal of the Association for Computing Machinery*, Vol. 8, October 1961, pp. 553-78.

21 ——. Indexing and abstracting by association. *American Documentation*, Vol. 13, No. 4, October 1962, pp. 378-90.

22 Vickery, B. C. *Classification and indexing in science*, 2nd edition, Butterworths, London, 1959, pp. 4-5.

23 ibid., p. 15.

24 Foskett, D. J. *Classification and indexing in the social sciences*, Butterworths, London, 1963, p. 80.

25 Maron, M. E. Automatic indexing: an experimental enquiry. *Journal of the Association for Computing Machinery*, Vol. 8, No. 3, July 1961, pp. 404-17.

26 Borko, H. and Bernick, M. D. *Automatic document*

classification. System Development Corporation, Technical Memorandum TM-771, 15th November, 1962.

27 Garvin, P. L. Some linguistic aspects of information retrieval. In The American University, Center for Technology and Administration, *Machine indexing: progress and problems. Papers presented at the Third Institute on Information Storage and Retrieval, February 13th–17th, 1961,* pp. 134-43.

28 Bohnert, L. M. New role of machines in document retrieval: definitions and scope. In The American University, Center for Technology and Administration, *Machine indexing: progress and problems. Papers presented at the Third Institute on Information Storage and Retrieval, February 13th–17th, 1961,* pp. 8-21.

29 Taube, M. *Computers and common sense: the myth of thinking machines,* Columbia University Press, New York, 1961, pp. 21-41.

30 Brenden, B. B. and Newkirk, H. W. Method for determining the thermal conductivity of incandescent solids. *Journal of Applied Physics,* Vol. 31, No. 4, April 1960, pp. 737-8.

31 Brinegar, C. S. Mark Twain and the Quintus Curtius Snodgrass letters: a statistical test of authorship. *Journal of the American Statistical Association,* Vol. 58, No. 301, March 1963, pp. 85-96.

9

Conclusion

In the first chapter of this book the view was expressed that the fundamental problem which is common to all information retrieval systems is that of providing for the nearest possible coincidence between the description of a subject by a searcher and the description used to enter documents on that subject in the system. Almost everything which has been said in the subsequent chapters has been aimed at helping to achieve that end.

Certain fundamental conclusions were reached as the argument progressed, the first one of which was that classification as applied in the conventional way, for the purpose of arranging things physically, must fail in those circumstances where different groupings are required at different times for different purposes. The magnitude of the problem was argued on a mathematical basis in chapter 4 and though the order of magnitude calculated there was extreme experience shows that the number of possible alternative arrangements is sufficiently large in some cases at least to militate strongly against the viability of classification-based systems.

The second conclusion was that when we leave aside classification and concern ourselves with subject specification, i.e. the making of classes by the use of groups of terms which together define those classes, we meet the problem of finding a given class in a system when we use at the time of searching only some of the terms which have been used to define that class at the time of input. This problem pervades not only the conventional alphabetical subject catalogue, but all pre-co-ordinate systems, including those based on classification.

The third important conclusion was that there is little we can do about the limitations concerning arrangement in classification, but that for the problem of retrieving specified information from any kind of system when we use only part of the total specification which was used when the information was entered in the system, we have the complete solution in the use of concept-co-ordination at the time of the search.

Much of the discussion on these aspects of the subject was concerned with the manipulation of terms and the question of the vocabularies which determine what those terms shall be was not discussed in any detail until chapter 6 was reached. Even when classification is considered in a fundamental way, we tend to concern ourselves a great deal with the manipulation of terms, as we do when we add or subtract terms to change the nature of classes. If the problem were as simple as this the information retrieval field would not find itself in the state of flux from which it suffers at the present time. What has been said in this book has depended largely on what is known and it is unfortunate that we know a great deal more about the mechanics of retrieval systems than we know about semantic analysis. Nevertheless we seem to move in a sea of confusion even where the more manageable aspects of the problem are concerned and it has been the purpose here to try to clarify the situation and in many cases this has involved the introduction of theory which is simple enough but which seems seldom to have existed consciously in the minds of the many practitioners in the information retrieval field.

When we have refined our systems from the point of view of the mechanics of handling terms, there remains this seemingly intractable problem of semantics. There seems to be little point in extending the machine facilities which are already available to us whilst we are still comparatively powerless to convert the ideas existing in human brains into language which meets all our needs whether it be used inside or outside a machine. Most of the books on information problems which are currently appearing are largely machine-oriented and into this category fall several which have appeared since the writing of this work was begun.[1, 2, 3] There is little doubt that research in the future should be aimed fairly and squarely at semantic analysis and it may be that work of the kind which Farradane has done, which is based on the psychology of human thought, and points a possible way to the reduction of thought processes to recognisable patterns, will prove to be the most fruitful kind of approach.[4]

There are a number of approaches to the problem of semantics in which there can be discerned what seems to be a common principle. This is the concept of synthesis in a very basic sort of way so that any kind of subject, regardless of its complexity, can be stated specifically and unambiguously by the combination of the necessary elemental entities. In chapter 6 the ideas of integrative levels, minimum vocabularies and semantic factoring were mentioned, and even in traditional classification the linking of genera and differences to give various levels of specificity follows the pattern. Clearly the stringency of the criteria relating to these several concepts varies greatly, as for instance between the seemingly impossible requirements of minimum vocabularies and the freedom permissible with semantic factoring, but if there is one conclusion which can be drawn from what has been said in the preceding chapters it is this: if we could reach the position wherein we had a vocabulary of terms which could be synthesised to meet any particular requirement in subject specification, and if there was only one way in which those terms could be used to provide any such subject specification, then such a vocabulary used with concept co-ordination for the purpose of providing maximum flexibility in manipulation would solve the retrieval problem completely. Reaching such a perfect state of affairs with regard to vocabulary is the fundamental problem and the more nearly we reach perfection the more we shall eliminate the present inevitable see-saw between recall and relevance, for what we do when we improve the quality of vocabulary is to push up one or the other, or both, and eliminate the depression of one when the other is increased.

Improvement in vocabulary quality starts with the simple process of eliminating synonyms. As far as positive control is concerned, this, together with the definition of terms in order to reach a state of mutual exclusion, and precautions such as links and roles to prevent false co-ordinations, is about as far as we go. We then introduce the 'see also' principle to try to cater for those terms which cannot be mutually exclusive (the extent to which this happens is to be seen clearly in modern retrieval thesauri) and from this point on we are at the mercy of language and its infinite variety of meaning. If we could devise means to utilise effectively the principle of synthesis of terms to meet all our needs we should eliminate the problem discussed in chapter 6 of 'what things are and what they are called', for we should have no doubt about the proper citation of a given subject, though we should have to treat quite rigorously the problem of what kind of definition was appropriate in a particular context and the several kinds of intension, which were also discussed in chapter 6, are relevant here. Apart from the removal of ambiguity we should simplify the problem of 'generic encoding' for a thing would become more or less generic by the removal or addition respectively of terms in a specification. The problem of providing for generic search, which so vexes post-co-ordinate systems, particularly those using elemental terms, would disappear, for the need to provide references would be eliminated when movement up or down a hierarchy was achieved by merely removing or adding one or more terms.

Work on the problems of semantics is likely to be of a long term nature, though Farradane claims already that his 'formalised method of expressing the relations which are the inner logic of our thinking has been found to be a basic tool for a variety of tasks'. He regards his method as 'the metalanguage for achieving accurate expression of knowledge without the ambiguities of ordinary language'.[5] This is certainly getting to the heart of the matter and as Farradane's concern is with relations, his methods are a promising way of providing for the problem of what Ullmann calls a 'semantic subdivision' of syntax, when he discusses the general question of 'units of relation'.[6] Farradane accepts the difficulties of standardising terminology for substantives and this promises to be a really serious problem unless substantives can be treated in a similar way to the relations expressed between them, for the use of terms changes with time and meaning is dependent on use for, as Ullmann says '. . . the meaning of a word can be ascertained *only* by studying its use. There is no short cut to meaning, through introspection or by any other method."[7]

Within the limits of our current knowledge, however, it does seem that more could be done to provide general guidance on the construction of vocabularies for post-co-ordinate systems for there is now a considerable body of experience by users of such systems. As discussed in chapter 6, it seems that the degree of telescoping of terms will be dictated by subject emphasis within a particular system, but it might be possible to do something, for instance about the forms of words which are used. Would it not be possible for instance to lay down rules which dictate whether the participial or gerundive forms are to be preferred to adjectives deriving from them, and that where a verb derives from a substantive the substantive is to take precedence over the verb and adjectives deriving from it? Thus we should have the term HEAT which would serve for the verb HEATING and for the adjective HEATED and perhaps HOT as well. Where a verb did not derive from the application or introduction of the substantive as is the case with HEATING, we should of course use the process term, e.g. MACHINING, which would still serve its derived adjective, i.e. MACHINED. It should also be possible to prescribe that an agent or a piece of equipment used for carrying out a process should be designated by its usual name, e.g. a HEATER, notwithstanding that HEAT is already used, or conversely the rule might be that a heater is described by the two terms HEAT (for HEATING) and EQUIPMENT. The desirability of using terms for both properties and specific properties rather than one or the other might also be considered, e.g. VISCOSITY and VISCOUS, OPACITY and OPAQUE. Adjectives deriving directly from substantives where a process term is unlikely to be used might be regarded as unsatisfactory and the substantive used instead, e.g. STRIPES for STRIPED, GROOVES for GROOVED.

It may be that there is no great significance in formalising terminology in this way but vocabulary building does seem to be simplified to some extent by having guiding principles to preferred word forms, even though some terms which normally would be suppressed have to be accepted in particular retrieval systems to meet the special needs of those systems. Where systems can be highly categorised these provisions may not be necessary because the categories will determine the form of the terms which they contain, but subject fields vary greatly in the degree to which they lend themselves to categorisation and where a vocabulary with a looser structure is required such rules may be helpful. The work of Coates in formulating rules for component order for alphabetical subject headings on the basis of the things and actions which the terms represent was discussed in chapter 3. It seems probable that work based on similar criteria, on the lines outlined above, for the purpose of determining word forms for concept-co-ordination systems would be well worthwhile.

Much of the work which is being reported currently is directed at the solution of problems actually encountered in devising retrieval systems for particular purposes, and it is clear that these specific problems are often capable of satisfactory solution. In the field of chemistry, for instance, it seems that it is possible to control information within limited areas with precision, but in other and wider fields the search for the underlying key to semantic control will need to be pursued with vigour, unless it can be shown that the problem of matching the searcher's requirements with the indexer's interpretation of a subject is capable of solution on an entirely different basis. The idea, discussed in chapter 8, of doing this on a purely statistical basis, using ordinary language as the material to be processed, does not seem very convincing at the present time, but on the results of the work done to date we have no justification for rejecting it as of no consequence.

After the theme of chapters 1 to 6, ending with the discussion of vocabulary control, the subjects of chapters 7 and 8 seem to be something of a digression. There are two reasons for considering the distinction between co-ordination and correlation (chapter 7) which seem to be compelling at the present time. Firstly, the subject of information retrieval is becoming more and more (and it seems dangerously) merged with all sorts of other information handling and processing techniques. Secondly, the word 'correlative' is being used as a substitute for 'co-ordinate' and as correlation is a subject quite separate from retrieval, and an important one in its own right, it was felt that it was the best example of a technique with which retrieval should not be confused. If we try to incorporate in a single system the facilities for all sorts of information handling, such as counting, summarising, calculating and correlating, we shall find ourselves doing a lot of things very badly and none, including information retrieval, very well. Typical of the introduction of these complexities into the field are the 'levels of treatment of information and data' detailed by Costello in a chapter whose subject is specifically 'indexing in depth', in a work entitled *Information handling: first principles*.[8] What is doubly disturbing about this is that not only is this irrelevancy introduced but the philosophy of the real subject of the chapter is so unconvincing. The incredible conclusion is reached that 'A deep index . . . is appreciably different from a co-ordinate index', though it had earlier been stated that 'A deep index is in a sense a specific type of index which employs the principles of concept co-ordination'. Far from trying to show the difference between a deep index and a co-ordinate index, it has been the purpose of part of the present work to show that a deep index must necessarily be a co-ordinate index.

The consideration of automatic indexing and automatic abstracting which formed the subject of chapter 8 was separated from the main theme because, whilst some of the issues are relevant to the matters discussed in the earlier chapters, the principles on which machine produced indexes, automatic classification, and full-text searching by machine are based are quite different if only because the work reported there is for the most part dependent upon statistical criteria. Thus, even if indexes as such are machine produced their compilation will be based on principles which are different from those used in manual indexing, whether the indexes be alphabetical or classified. Full-text searching is of course still further removed from conventional indexing, even though the criteria be similar to those used for auto-indexing. A book on information retrieval would be incomplete without reference to these techniques, for though they cannot be considered as part of the theme of chapters 1 to 6 of this work, it may be that at some future time they will supersede these established techniques.

It is felt that what has been said in this book comprises a major part of the subject referred to as 'information retrieval'. The literature on the subject currently ranges from the most elementary treatment such as the popular article on co-ordinate principles applied in manual systems to the most advanced theorising such as the highly mathematical treatise on textual analysis. There are currently no criteria by which the relevance of the many approaches can be judged but no reasonably promising line of enquiry should be ignored. However, until such time as there is reason to believe that a significantly better system has been discovered, we should do all we can to exploit established methods. The best use of available knowledge on the subject can be made only if the principles on which existing and proposed systems operate are fully understood. It has been the purpose of this book to try to contribute to that understanding in order that the theories might be put to better use. If it helps only in our having better reasons for doing what we do, it will have served its purpose, for choice of methods need not then be entirely a matter of chance and the potential for reaching out successfully still further is thus enhanced.

REFERENCES

1   Becker, J. and Hayes, R. M. *Information storage and retrieval: tools, elements, theories*, Wiley, New York, 1963.
2   Bourne, C. P. *Methods of information handling*, Wiley, New York, 1963.
3   Howerton, P. W. (ed.) *Information handling: first principles*, Spartan Books, Washington, 1963.

4   Farradane, J. Relational indexing and classification in the
    light of recent experimental work in psychology. *In-
    formation Storage and Retrieval*, Vol. 1, No. 1, January–
    March 1963, pp. 3-11.
5   ibid., p. 6.
6   Ullmann, S. *Semantics: an introduction to the science of
    meaning*, Blackwell, Oxford, 1962, pp. 32-3.
7   ibid., p. 67.
8   Costello, J. C. Indexing in depth: practical parameters.
    In *Information handling: first principles*, edited by P. W.
    Howerton, Spartan Books, Washington, 1963, pp. 55-87.

Appendix

Description of the method of producing the SLIC index at British Nylon Spinners Limited

The experimental index mentioned in chapter 4 is based on the principles discussed there of deriving every combination of terms from the set of alphabetically ordered terms assigned by the indexer, selecting from these combinations only those which do not form the beginnings of longer combinations, and listing these selected groups in alphabetical order. For this reason the index is referred to as a SLIC index (Selective Listing In Combination). The maximum number of terms which may be assigned as a set by the indexer is 5, the formula giving a total of 16 entries for such a set, though where the nature of a document justifies it more than one set of terms may be assigned. The procedure is as follows:

1   The documents to be indexed are entered in an 'accessions register' for the purpose of assigning to each a unique number. This follows the usual practice for post-co-ordinate term-entry retrieval systems and provides for the identification of a document by reference to the register when the number has been thrown up in a search.

2   An indexing slip is made out for each document and the information entered on it consists of the set or sets of terms assigned by the indexer and the document's accession number. The terms in each set are entered on the slip in alphabetical order, e.g. a document numbered 1374 on the effect of cooling air temperature on the rate of crystallisation of nylon would be entered thus:

AIR: COOLING: CRYSTALLISING: SPEEDS:
TEMPERATURE   1374

3   Each set of terms is transferred to a standard 80-column
IBM card in the order in which it is presented, together
with the accession number, the card being divided into
five fields of 15 columns each (one field for each of the
terms) and one field of 5 columns (for the accession
number). Because of the limitation of field size, no term
of more than 14 characters is admitted to the index.
This ensures that a space always exists between any
pair of terms in a set because column 15 in each field
is always unused.

The card for the above subject, with the punchings 'in-

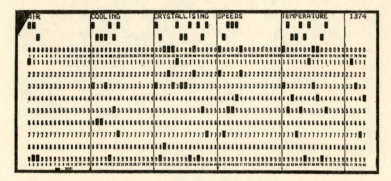

Fig 12 A 'primary card' for the SLIC index

terpreted' in printed characters at the top would appear
as in figure 12. In some cases there are less than five
terms in a set and for convenience in later processing
the cards are kept in separate batches of 5-term cards, 4-
term cards, etc. These cards are termed the 'primary'
cards.

4   It is now necessary to produce 15 other cards from each
primary card in order to provide the total of 16 combinations of terms which are to appear in the printed
index. These additional 15 cards will all be referred to
as 'secondary' cards. Using the letters A, B, C, D and E
to represent the terms, the full list of entries for a 5-

term set is as follows, the first group being the original set assigned by the indexer and thus the set forming the primary card:

A B C D E
A B C E
A B D E
A B E
A C D E
A C E
A D E
A E
B C D E
B C E
B D E
B E
C D E
C E
D E
E

The secondary cards are prepared by the use of a reproducing punch. The first batch of secondaries is produced by wiring the punch so that when a primary card with the terms A B C D E is fed to it a new card which reads A B C E is punched. This requires that columns 1–45 of the primary card are reproduced in columns 1–45 of the secondary card, columns 46–60 are not reproduced, and columns 61–75 of the primary are reproduced in columns 46–60 of the secondary card. This is simply a matter of wiring the columns of the reading head of the punch to the appropriate columns of the punching mechanism. Columns 76–80, which represent the accession number, are of course always reproduced in columns 76–80 of the secondary card. With the punch so wired, all the 5-term primary cards are fed through and the first secondary card for each is produced. The card shown in figure 12 would produce a secondary card which would appear as shown in figure 13.

The punch is now rewired to produce the third combination shown in the list, i.e. A B D E, and the second batch of secondary cards is reproduced from the primaries. This procedure could be repeated until all the 16 cards for each 5-term entry were prepared, but this would not take into account the punching of secondary cards for those primaries which comprised only 4, 3, or 2 terms, i.e. those deriving from sets in which the indexer had not used the maximum of 5 terms. It would be uneconomical to re-wire the punch for each of these

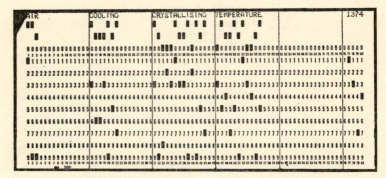

Fig 13 A 'secondary card' for the SLIC index

series all over again, so the following procedure is adopted.

When the last secondary card to bear 4 terms has been punched from the 5-term primaries (i.e. the card B C D E, item 9 in the list), the original primary card of 5 terms is abandoned as primary card and this newly-punched 4-term card is substituted for it. All the primary cards emanating from the 4-term sets assigned by the indexer are now added to the 4-term secondaries and re-wiring and punching are continued until the 13th entry is reached when the procedure is repeated in order to introduce the 3-term primaries. Finally the 2-term primary cards are introduced in the same way at the 15th combination. (It will be noted that the change occurs each time a new term comes up to the front for entry word.)

5 The whole file of punched cards is sorted into strict alphabetical order. Cards bearing the same combination of terms are sorted into numerical order by accession number.

6 The cards are fed to the IBM 1401 computer for the purpose of printing out the index. The computer is programmed to print any set of terms once only and to subsume to that set all the accession numbers which apply to it. Thus if a batch of 20 cards is encountered, all of which bear the same set of terms, the computer will print the terms from the first card only and will ignore everything on the other 19 cards except the accession numbers.

Where more than one set of terms has been assigned to one document by the indexer and some terms are common to two or more sets there will be cases in the secondary cards where a given number will be subsumed more than once to a given combination of terms. The computer is programmed to suppress all but the first occurrence of a number in such cases.

7 The computer prints out directly on to paper mats for use on an offset-litho machine and the requisite number of copies of the index are now run off. A sample of the finished index is shown in figure 14.

Each holder of the index is supplied with three separate items:

(1.) A copy of the dictionary of approved terms
(2.) A copy of the index proper
(3.) A copy of the accessions register.

He also receives a copy of the instructions for use of the index and these are worded as follows:

(a) Select from the dictionary those terms which you feel best describe the subject of your search. You will be

MEMORANDA INDEX   PAGE 93

KNITTING	WARPING	WRAPPING			
1345					
KNITTING	WARPING	YARNS			
101 763		945 1181 1452 1565			
KNITTING	WARPING	30 DENIER			
901					
KNITTING	WEAVING				
1370 1801					
KNITTING	WEAVING	YARNS			
763					
KNITTING	WEFT				
1391 1672					
KNITTING	WELDING				
7					
KNITTING	WELTS				
1398					
KNITTING	WORSTED				
1272					
KNITTING	WRAPPING				
1345					
KNITTING	YARNS				
69 101 122 164 763 772 885 886 945 979 1113 1151 1173 1181 1268					
1379 1396 1411 1452 1565 1620 1664					
KNITTING	YARNS	6 DENIER			
1516					
KNITTING	YARNS	15 DENIER			
727 1616 1620					
KNITTING	6 DENIER				
1516					
KNITTING	15 DENIER				
727 956 959 1371 1374 1616 1620 1631					
KNITTING	30 DENIER				
901					
KNOTS	POLYMERS	STRENGTH	TWINES	VISCOSITY	
1454					
KNOTS	POLYMERS	STRENGTH	VISCOSITY		
1454					
KNOTS	POLYMERS	TWINES	VISCOSITY		
1454					
KNOTS	POLYMERS	VISCOSITY			
1454					
KNOTS	RATIOS	ROPES	TENACITY		
1387					
KNOTS	RATIOS	STRENGTH	TWINES		
1454					
KNOTS	RATIOS	TENACITY			
1387					
KNOTS	RATIOS	TWINES			
1454					
KNOTS	ROPES	TENACITY			
1387					
KNOTS	SLIPPING	WETTING			
1438					
KNOTS	STRENGTH	TESTING	TWINES		
1438					
KNOTS	STRENGTH	TWINES			
1438 1454					
KNOTS	STRENGTH	TWINES	VISCOSITY		
1454					
KNOTS	STRENGTH	VISCOSITY			
1454					
KNOTS	TENACITY				
1387					
KNOTS	TESTING	TWINES			
1438					
KNOTS	TWINES				
1438 1454					
KNOTS	TWINES	VISCOSITY			
1454					
KNOTS	VISCOSITY				
1454					
KNOTS	WETTING				
1438					
KRALASTIC	SLEEVES	SNATCHING	TAKE OFF	TENSION	
1172					
KRALASTIC	SLEEVES	SNATCHING	TENSION		
1172					
KRALASTIC	SLEEVES	TAKE OFF	TENSION		
119 1172					
KRALASTIC	SLEEVES	TENSION			
119 1172					
KRALASTIC	SNATCHING	TAKE OFF	TENSION		
1172					

Fig 14 A sample of the finished SLIC index

guided in this by 'see' references from non-standard terms to approved alternatives and also by suggestions in the form of 'see also' references. The number of terms must not exceed 5, and it is better to start with too few rather than too many terms, for it is easy to narrow down your search if the result of your first attempt is too long a list of document numbers.

(b)   Arrange your selected terms in alphabetical order, e.g.

BOBBINS :   SURFACES :   TAKE-OFF

and consult this group in the alphabetical sequence of the index. Take into account not only this particular heading, but those headings also which comprise these terms plus other terms which follow, e.g.

BOBBINS :   SURFACES :   TAKE-OFF :   TENSION :
UNIFORMITY
BOBBINS :   SURFACES :   TAKE-OFF :   TYRE CORDS

(c)   List the numbers found under these headings and consult the accessions register (which is arranged in order of these numbers) to determine the identity of the relevant documents. In some cases you will find that a given number repeats itself under several of the headings which you are using. Once you have noted the number, all other citations of it can of course be ignored.

(d)   If the number of documents listed seems to be excessive, narrow your search by either:

   (i)   taking into account other terms which you see following your group of selected terms in a heading (more likely to be useful with entries at the beginning of the index) or,

   (ii) thinking of another term to add to your selected group, either at its beginning or between other terms, and consulting the newly-formed group at the appropriate point in the index (more likely to be useful with entries towards the end of the index).

It was mentioned in chapter 4 that there are certain difficulties which arise in the practical use of an index such as
this. These are implicit in sections (c) and (d) of the instructions for use above. Firstly, the unwanted repetition of a given
document number under the several headings comprising the
block of entries being consulted may be something of an
irritation. This is the price of reducing the size of the index
to about half of what it would need to be to avoid the problem
(i.e. from $2^n - 1$ entries to $2^{(n-1)}$). The second feature which
may cause difficulty is the difference between the nature
of the headings towards the beginning of the index, where
headings tend towards the maximum length of five terms,
and the nature of those towards the end of the sequence,
where the tendency is towards the minimum length of one
term only.

The degree to which these features militate against the
effectiveness of the index is yet to be shown by experience,
but there is no reason to believe that the problems will be
serious. Indeed it remains to be seen how much advantage
might accrue from the introduction of a certain amount of
'browsability' into a co-ordinate index. No less interesting
is the possibility that a technique might be developed for re-
introducing the principle of number-matching as with Uniterm cards. This might be a very powerful technique, for
theoretically it is possible to co-ordinate up to ten terms by
matching but one pair of numbers.

These ideas are, however, speculation and the important
features of the index as far as its present intended purpose
is concerned are:

(a)   Within the limits of the 5-term maximum length of
       subject designation, concept co-ordination is as posi-
       tive as it is with special equipment such as optical
       stencil cards.

(b)   Its particular advantage is that any number of copies
       can be produced at low cost.

(c)   It is capable of up-dating at frequent intervals. (The
       intention is to up-date every twelve months.)

(d) There is absolutely no maintenance required by the
     holder of a copy. Each holder will be supplied with an
     up-dated (i.e. cumulated) index every year and his old
     copy will be scrapped.

There are, of course, methods of manipulating the data to
produce the desired result other than those described above,
but this account has been presented in this way in order to
provide a clear picture of the procedure. It is possible in fact
to assign all the work to a computer if the machine's facilities
are adequate. The IBM 1401 used by British Nylon Spinners
is in its present form not able to perform the entire operation, but certain techniques are being used to avoid the use
of a reproducing punch and to reduce the time necessary
for machine-sorting the cards into alphabetical order. Even
with the fastest machinery the latter process is a lengthy one
because of the need to sort on nearly all 80 columns.

Index